"In cities like Rome, Venice, or Florence, beauty is obvious. It's an exact match to the postcards and the social media posts, and the takeaway is pretty much the same for everyone. You can delight in these places, even as a passive observer. But not Sicily. Nobody's a bystander here. If you're here, you're in the game." So writes Victoria Granof in this loving tribute to Sicilian sweets past and present.

Sicilian pastries are fanciful, bawdy, and brash. They are celebratory, superstitious, and some of the most show-stopping desserts around. Luckily, they are also quite easy to make at home now that Sicilian pistachios, sheep's milk ricotta, jasmine water, fragrant lemons, and fennel are easier than ever to procure. In Victoria Granof's expert hands, readers learn to make Meyer Lemon and Bay Leaf Gelato; Schiumone, a frozen mousse of jasmine-scented almond milk; Gela di Melone, a fruit pudding of white melon and orange blossom; and Pasticcini di Pistacchio Con Gelsomino, pistachio and jasmine macarons. Full of gorgeous food and location photography, sharp and funny headnotes, and expert recipes, *Sicily, My Sweet* will transport and delight.

◆◆◆

Scorning the table of drinks, glittering with crystal and silver on the right, he moved left toward that of the sweetmeats. Huge blond babas, Mont Blancs snowy with whipped cream, cakes speckled with white almonds and green pistachio nuts, hillocks of chocolate-covered pastry, brown and rich as the topsoil of the Catanian plain from which, in fact, through many a twist and turn they had come; pink ices, champagne ices, coffee ices, all parfaits, which fell apart with a squelch as the knife cleft them, melody in major of crystallized cherries, acid notes of yellow pineapple, and those cakes called "triumphs of gluttony" filled with green pistachio paste, and shameless "virgin's cakes" shaped like breasts. Don Fabrizio asked for some of these and, as he held them in his plate, looked like a profane caricature of St. Agatha. "Why ever didn't the Holy Office forbid these cakes when it had the chance? St. Agatha's sliced-off breasts sold by convents, devoured at dances! Well, well!"

GIUSEPPE TOMASI DI LAMPEDUSA
THE LEOPARD

Sicily,

MY SWEET

VICTORIA
GRANOF

Love Notes to an Island, with Recipes for Cakes, Cookies, Puddings, and Preserves

Hardie Grant
NORTH AMERICA

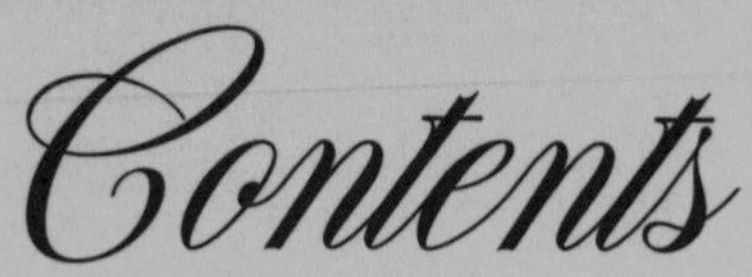

INTRODUCTION

Sicily, My Sweet

7

SICILIA

An Island Ravished

16

LA DISPENSA

The Pantry

21

A Occhio—Baking by Eye 26

Pistacchi di Bronte—Bronte Pistachios 27

BISCOTTI DEL MATTINO

Morning Cookies

31

BISCOTTI DA RIPOSTO

Keeping Cookies

41

PASTICCINI DI MANDORLE E PISTACCHI

Almond & Pistachio Sweets

57

Frutta Martorana—Fruits to Fool the Bishop. Or the King. 58

DOLCETTI RIPIENI

Filled Pastries

81

Cioccolato Di Modica—Modican Chocolate 100

CANNOLI E I SUOI AMICI

Cannoli & Friends

105

Unholy Cannoli 110
Dolci di Badia—Convent Sweets 120
Il Trionfo di Gola—A Triumph of Gluttony 125

TORTE E CROSTATE

Cakes & Tarts

127

Cassata 128

LIEVITATI E FRITTI

Yeasted & Fried

147

DOLCI AL CUCCHIAIO

Spoon Sweets & Fillings

163

GELATI E GRANITE

Frozen Sweets

177

How to Order Gelati in Sicily 190
Then There's Granita 193

CONSERVE E CROCCANTI

Preserves & Candy

195

BEVANDE E LIQUORI

Drinks & Liqueurs

219

Acknowledgments 233
Index 234

Sicily, My Sweet

I keep a sesame biscotto in my freezer that is going on fourteen years old. It was from the last batch made by my nonna. Keeping that frozen braid of lemon-scented flour, oil, sugar, and eggs near, somehow keeps *her* near. I sense her hands when mine roll and twist that same dough into those same braids, and her voice calling me by the pet name only she used: *Vituccia!* (*-uccia* is an endearment tacked on to the end of a name). It is my name, my nonna's name, and her nonna's name.

On my mother's side of the family, we are Sephardic Jews from Sicily. We were there 2,000 years ago, when Greeks brought honey and almonds to the island. We were there during the Golden Age of Islam, when the Arabs brought over sugar and flower essences and made ices and ice creams. We were there when a brief French occupation brought with it *bignè,* and brioche; and when Sicily became part of the Spanish Empire, chocolate made its way back from Mexico with the conquistadors and into Sicilian sweets.

And then, it all came to a painful end with the Spanish Inquisition.

On March 31, 1492, King Ferdinand and Queen Isabella issued the Alhambra Decree, ordering the expulsion of all Jews from the Crowns of Castile and Aragon and their territories by July 31 of that year. Three days later, they sent Columbus off to discover a westward route to India.

From Sicily, we fled to the Ottoman Empire, taking our language, religion, and foodways with us.

That was half a millennium ago, and the memories that remain of the Old, Old Country are sense memories, mostly: the aroma of anise-scented yeast breads embedded with a hardboiled egg, crunchy breakfast biscotti showered with sesame seeds, quince and rose spoon sweets, candied kumquats sewn together with thread, and a wheatberry porridge made by whoever spots a baby's first tooth. Sugar makes Sicilians happy, and these are sticky memories indeed.

Apart from the sweets, the language, and familial grudges that will be taken to the grave, our Sicilian-ness was eclipsed by the past few centuries in the former Ottoman Empire. Or so I thought. When the pull to connect those sense memories to a place became insistent, I traveled to Turkey. It was beautiful, but it wasn't *home*.

In 1995, I was working as a pastry chef at Smashbox Studios in Los Angeles. Someone had left a *Gourmet* magazine in our kitchen with an article

◆◆◆

about Sicilian pastry cook Maria Grammatico. Ms. Grammatico, now in her eighties, had spent her childhood in a convent in the mountaintop town of Erice, on Sicily's western side. There, from the age of eleven, she was taught the art of pastry-making by the nuns of San Carlo. In the early 1960s, she opened her own shop in the same town, continuing the tradition she'd learned from the nuns. (Her shop is still there, and so is she.) In the article, she lamented the fact that few young people wanted to learn the art of pastry-making and voiced her fear that the tradition would soon be lost. *Who would carry it on?* she worried.

Maybe me? I thought.

That's what brought me to Sicily. I had visited other parts of Italy (there was one time, before the Internet, when I spent an entire month with a family I thought was mine but who I later discovered weren't even a *little* bit related) but had never ventured farther south than Naples. This time, landing at the airport in Catania, I found that it smelled like coffee, almonds, lemon, and cinnamon—and, somewhere in my sense memory, of home.

That's when I fell under Sicily's spell, in all her maddening, delicious, surreal glory. Turns out you can take a girl out of Sicily, but it takes more than a few centuries to take Sicily out of the girl.

In cities like Rome, Venice, or Florence, beauty is obvious. It's an exact match to the postcards and the social media posts, and the takeaway is pretty much the same for everyone. You can delight in these places, even as a passive observer.

But not Sicily.

Nobody's a bystander here. If you're here, you're in the game.

On one trip, my luggage was lost, our taxi driver tendered a lowball offer for my pretty teenage goddaughter, and we ate boiled weeds for dinner. We awoke the next morning to an *infiorata** outside our door; my luggage arrived on the shoulder of a Vespa driver named Massimo; and my goddaughter's virtue remained intact. I happily eat boiled weeds whenever I can now.

Sicily has a way of tossing you around before it lays jewels at your feet.

She is not curated. Her charms are not always immediately obvious. Sicily is a place designed for exploration, discovery, and, as it happens, exploitation.

Whatever you're seeking, you'll find here: Greek theaters; Roman mosaics; Byzantine, Norman, and baroque churches; 3,000-year-old saltworks (still in use) populated by flocks of pink flamingos; the oldest *mikvah* in Europe; outdoor markets dating back to the Arab occupation of the ninth century; hectares of citrus, pistachio, and almond groves; dramatic cliffs; black sand beaches; crystal-clear waters; long lunches in lush citrus groves; ski runs on an active volcano; brioche and granita at seaside cafes; the glamour of Taormina; the Baroque splendor of Catania; peace and quiet; food and wine; fast cars, fashion, art, and film; starry nights and illicit love.

* **The word *infiorata* means "covered in flowers."** For a few days each May and June, streets in the Sicilian towns of Noto and Taormina are blanketed with tapestries created entirely of flower petals to celebrate the coming of spring and the Feast of Corpus Domini.

◆◆◆

You'll also see crumbling *palazzi*, the skeletal remains of abandoned buildings, hookers strolling coastal roads, and multicolored bags of household trash left in piles right out in the open. Like I said—if you're here, you're in the game.

The poet Goethe said that the key to all of Italy is found in Sicily.

Sometime after that first trip, I moved from Los Angeles to New York and began my career as a food stylist. Working with publisher Judith Regan, who herself has Sicilian roots, led to the publication of my first book on Sicilian sweets. That was twenty-odd years ago, and all the pastry chefs I spoke to then were, like Maria Grammatico, afraid the traditions would die with them. The next generation no longer wanted to toil in obscurity for long hours and modest wages, churning out handmade pastries one by one. They were leaving the small towns for the big cities.

This was before the full flowering of the Internet. Food media was limited to magazines and a handful of cooking shows on public television; chefs like Bobby Flay, Gordon Ramsey, and Curtis Stone were cooking in restaurants for a living.

All these years later, the changes in Sicilian food culture—especially in that of her sweets—are happening quickly. This has everything to do with the most recent conqueror to breach Sicily's shores: the Internet. With it came camera phones, online platforms, and social media. Sicily has seen the Neolithic Age, the Iron Age, and the Industrial Age—and now, the Digital Age.

Online platforms, food blogs, and social media have become virtual meeting places for pastry enthusiasts to share recipes, ideas, videos, and images designed to make us drool and crave and want more. As a food stylist and commercial director, I've been on the front lines of the movement, which I find exciting for the most part. As someone who loves Sicily and her sweets, I find it heartening that the Internet has provided places for Sicilian pastry cooks to showcase their creations to a global audience without ever leaving home or abandoning tradition. To see gorgeous images of cannoli, *cassata, granite, gelati,* virgin's breasts, and triumphs of gluttony shared online is to immediately appreciate the artistry and craftsmanship of Sicilian pastries. This exposure has not only elevated the status of Sicilian pastries and pastry chefs around the world but has also encouraged experimentation and innovation.

It seems nearly every *pasticciere* in the land has fallen under the spell of the silicone mold. Everywhere you go, there are half-rounds and pyramids of *monoporzione* mousse-like creations that are indistinguishable from their counterparts in French, American, or Japanese pastry shops. My first response was intense disapproval, as though my traditional Sicilian toy doll was suddenly wearing stilettos and a sundress. But looking past the hacky shapes, I found traditional Sicilian ingredients, sometimes playing in coquettish combination with one another, and sometimes with flavors

CALAMITE

◆◆◆

new to Sicilian palates. (I'm looking at you, turmeric and curry powder.)

Also in proliferation are gelaterias with cartoonish décor, silly names, and all the charm of suburban strip malls (here's one area where globalization may not be such a good thing). Although I would never recommend one of these over the glut of good traditional gelaterias (look for the word *artigianale* on the sign), not all of them are trafficking in bubble gum gelato that comes from a mix. Caveat emptor.

Amidst the digital invasion, Sicilian sweets have managed to retain their essence and authenticity. Generations' worth of traditional recipes and techniques continue to be followed and cherished. The Internet hasn't replaced the traditions, but instead has called attention to them, providing a platform for innovation while honoring the rich heritage of Sicilian sweets. It's in this spirit that I've gone about creating this book.

I wanted the book to be about the past, present, and foreseeable future of Sicilian sweets. While it goes deeper into the territory I explored in my first book, this is by no means a scholarly tome. Rather, it's a very personal book about a place I love and the sweet things I've discovered there.

All those foreign invasions, conquests, and dominations left a complex and delicious imprint on Sicilian sweets, from Baroque almond cakes and pastries created by cloistered nuns to exquisite frozen confections first crafted by Arab invaders with snow from Mount Etna. Here I've gathered dozens of traditional recipes from convents, pastry shops, family, friends, and friends of friends, along with others that I have created in the spirit of this bewitching place. My hope is that if you like to bake, you'll bake from my book; and that if you don't, you'll enjoy its pretty pictures; and that if I whet your appetite for Sicily, you will go there, taste the sweets, and discover her beauty for yourself.

Remember, there are no bystanders in Sicily. If you're here, you're in the game. And what a sweet game it is!

specialità
granita
siciliana

AN ISLAND RAVISHED

◆◆◆

Ask a Sicilian what the origin of a pastry is, and the reply will be either *"gli Arabi,"* the Arabs; *"i Greci,"* the Greeks; or *"dall'Ottocento,"* the high-baroque period of the 1700s. While the effects of these three periods in Sicilian history are most immediately evident in Sicily's sweets, the story is a bit spicier. The largest island in the Mediterranean, with a strategic location at the crossroads of Europe and Africa, Sicily has been lusted after and lorded over by many suitors, all aiming to have their way with her. Repeated invasions, exploitations, dominations, and occupations have only served to add texture and depth to her allure.

Prior to 1000 BCE The Siculi, the Sicani, and the Elymi are the first known inhabitants of Sicily.

800 BCE Phoenicians—seafaring traders from present-day Lebanon—establish the first trading colonies in western Sicily.

Carthaginians from present-day Tunis in North Africa establish a colony in Mozia, a small island across from Marsala in western Sicily. There, they develop a salt industry, still in operation today, that extends to nearby areas around Trapani. Also in Mozia, the Carthaginians plant vineyards with wine grapes traded with Greece.

735 BCE The first Greek colony is established at Siracusa in eastern Sicily by Greeks from Corinth. The Greeks introduce the *hortus,* or kitchen garden. They bring olives, apiculture, hazelnuts, walnuts, pomegranates, more grapes, and figs, and develop a method for drying figs in the sun. Durum wheat is planted. They introduce cheese-making, and ricotta enters the scene.

200 BCE Sicily becomes a battleground in the Punic Wars between Rome and Carthage. The Romans emerge victorious, and Sicily becomes the first Roman province. Exports of wheat and barley from Sicily lead to mass exploitation and corruption under the newly formed feudal system. Sicily's nickname, the Granary of Rome, is a hard-won moniker.

Cherries, plums, and citrons are imported from Asia.

491 CE The Goths assume control of Sicily, uniting it with the Ostrogothic Kingdom of Italy.

535 CE Sicily is annexed to the Byzantine Empire. With that come cinnamon and cloves.

827 CE Arabs land at Mazara del Vallo in southwestern Sicily to begin their conquest of Sicily.

902 CE Conquest achieved, the Arabs begin to plant apricots, melons, rice, bananas, mulberries, date palms, pistachios, almonds, watermelon, and sugarcane. They also plant citrus orchards—called "gardens"—as places for relaxation and socializing.

Flower essences (rose water, jasmine, and orange-blossom water), along with sesame, saffron, and raisins, enter the Sicilian kitchen. Sicilian Arabs devise a method for making ice-based desserts with the snow from Mount Etna. Innovations in irrigation mean that agriculture flourishes, while feudal estates flounder.

Coffee arrives from Ethiopia.

1060 CE	The Norman Conquest of Sicily begins when frenchified Vikings invade from their base in Normandy, France. Butter becomes the cooking fat of choice in aristocratic households. Apples and pears are planted in high mountain altitudes.
1068 CE	The Norman Conquest of Sicily is complete. Knights are given large feudal estates for their loyalty and military service. They are designated barons and become the first Sicilian nobility. Blue eyes enter the Sicilian gene pool.
1189 CE	Childless, William II designates his aunt Constance as his heir. Norman rule ends when Henry IV of Swabia (in today's Germany) claims the throne on behalf of his wife, Constance.
1208 CE	Frederick II ascends the throne. Red hair enters the Sicilian gene pool.
1268–82 CE	The brief period of French rule ends with the popular uprising known as the Sicilian Vespers.
1302 CE	The Treaty of Caltabellotta gives control of Sicily to Spain under the crown of Aragon. Spain will be the last great contributor to Sicilian cuisine. The sugar industry thrives in the hands of Sicily's Jews.
1492 CE	The Spanish Inquisition forces the expulsion of the ancient community of Jews from Sicily. Without them, the island's thriving centuries-old sugar industry collapses.
1503 CE	The Age of Exploration of the New World begins under the Catholic kings of Spain. Spanish galleons bring chocolate, vanilla, squash, tomatoes, peppers, and cactus to Sicily.
1535 CE	Pastry-making enters convent kitchens. Sicily's nobility begins feasting on chancellor's buttocks and virgin's breasts.
1713–34 CE	For a brief period, Sicily is first under (unremarkable) Savoyard rule, then Austrian rule.
1734 CE	Bourbon King Charles claims the throne on behalf of Spain. The aristocracy dominates daily life.
1767 CE	Charles's son Ferdinand inherits the throne of Sicily. He rules alongside his Austrian wife, Maria Carolina, sister to Marie Antoinette, from their court in Naples.
1799 CE	Circumstances of the Napoleonic Wars cause the royal court to relocate to Palermo. French chefs, called *monsù*—a corruption of the word *monsieur*—are imported, to cater to the tastes of the Austrian queen. The aristocracy hire monsù of their own and eat very well. Swiss pastry chefs arrive in Sicily to set up shop in Palermo and Catania.
1816 CE	The kingdoms of Naples and Sicily are united to form the Kingdom of the Two Sicilies.
1860 CE	Sicily is liberated from Spanish rule when Giuseppe Garibaldi and his militia of 1,000 "Redshirts" win a populist revolt against the Bourbon government.
1861 CE	The Kingdom of the Two Sicilies is unified with Italy.

PASTICCERIA SVIZZERA
A. Caviezel & C.
CATANIA
Zucchero
semolato

3 grams)

CLASSICO
TWININGS
English Breakfast Tea
PELLICOLA
Alluminio
PANEANGELI
Amido di Mais
PANEANGELI
"LIEVITO PANE degli ANGELI"
CANNELLA
AMMONIACA
per dolci
FARINE
SELEZIONE
DENTI
FARINA DI
GRANO TENERO
TIPO "00"
BICARBONATO
MULINO S. CROCE
& GIOVANNI DI MARTINO S.R.L.

THE PANTRY
La Dispensa

Flours

FARINE

One day, walking into town from the outskirts of Modica, I came upon a small flour mill with a roll-up door, open to the street. At Molino di Santa Maria, they've been milling ancient Sicilian grains into flour in small batches since 1918. Davide, one of the two cousins and a brother who own this mill, told me there used to be a stream running through the town, giving the district the nickname *Venezia del Sud*, or Venice of the South. Several watermills on its banks milled flour on ancient grindstones. Water gave way to electricity in the 1940s, then the '70s saw the stream cemented over to build nondescript blocks of homes. Most of the mills disappeared or moved. Their Russello flour is superior to any flour I've baked with so far. You can almost taste the earth it was grown in.

In the United States, flour is graded according to protein content, while in Italy, it is graded by how finely it's milled. This can make substitutions tricky in some cases, so here are some general guidelines.

00 Flour

00—or *doppio zero*—flour is made from soft durum wheat and is the finest grind among Italian wheat flours. It's comparable to American all-purpose flour and can be used in the same way. Note that 00 flour absorbs less liquid, so use 2 tablespoons less per cup of 00 flour than all-purpose flour. It's available in most large supermarkets, Italian and international groceries, and online.

0 Flour

Sometimes called Manitoba flour, 0 flour is milled less finely than 00 flour and has a higher protein content. This makes it a stronger flour, good for yeasted baked goods and those that need more structure. It is comparable to American bread flour. Use in equal amounts as bread flour. It's not widely available outside of Italy, but you can buy it online.

Cake Flour

Cake flour is an American product, and there really is no comparable flour in Sicily. It has the lowest protein content of all flours and is very finely milled, making it good for light, fluffy cakes. If you don't have cake flour, replace 2 tablespoons per 1 cup (120 g) of all-purpose flour with cornstarch.

Semolina Flours

These are beautiful yellow flours made from hard durum wheat. The coarser grind, called *semola,* is usually sold as semolina or semolina flour in the United States. It is good for bread and pasta. *Semola rimacinata* is a finer grind that adds a lovely sandy texture and yellow color to cookies and pastry dough.

Almond and Pistachio Flours

These are very finely milled nuts, nothing else. Make sure you buy them from a good source that has a quick turnover, since they can become rancid and lose moisture quickly.

Fats

GRASSI

Lard, Butter, and Shortening

Lard (*sugna*) has long been the principal fat in Sicilian baking. Pigs were everywhere, so their fat was cheap. Lard gives baked goods a light, crumbly texture, and when used for frying it produces a crispness that some think is better than oil. (I confess I can't tell the difference between the cannoli shells fried in oil and those fried in lard.) If you buy it fresh, or from an artisanal source, it doesn't taste a bit piggy.

The Normans brought their love of butter to Sicily in the eleventh century, but it was only really available to affluent households who had access to cows. Butter is now easily accessible and widely used.

Then there's shortening (*strutto*), which I wouldn't recommend; it's often a mixture of lard and hydrogenated fat, which is good for nobody and leaves an unpleasant coating on the tongue.

Oils for Frying

I am not a food scientist, but I do know what works.

Sicilians have fried pastries in olive oil for centuries. Not brand-new freshly pressed olive oil with its big, bold, zingy flavors, but "last year's" oil, when those big flavors have mellowed and become less assertive. For every oil, there is a season and a purpose. Speaking of olive oil, never buy "light" olive oil, even though you may think its light color and mild flavor would be better for frying; it's nothing but chemically processed, ultra-refined olive oil. *Olio di semi*, or seed oil—most often sunflower—is another good oil for frying, followed by canola oil.

Tropical Oils and Vegan Butter

I'm surprised by how many vegans there are in Sicily. As their ranks grow, so—I predict—will the popularity of coconut oil, palm oil, and vegan butter (essentially margarine). I tested some of the recipes in this book with *refined* coconut oil and with shortening made from palm and coconut oils; they work, and no coconut flavor comes through with either one. Vegan butter works just as well as real butter and keeps its flavor to itself.

Salt

SALE

I used fine sea salt for all the recipes in this book. In Trapani, on Sicily's west coast, seawater is gathered in *saline*, or salt pans, much as the Phoenicians did 2,700 years ago. With little more than the hot sun and sirocco winds from Africa, it becomes the deliciously briny *sale marino* (sea salt) that I use.

Leavening

LIEVITO

Baking Powder

In Sicily, baking powder flavored with a bit of vanillin is called *lievito per dolci*, and it comes in packets of 1 tablespoon. Pane degli Angeli is the most well-known brand—so much so that, in the same way facial tissues are called Kleenex, any brand of baking powder will be called Pane degli Angeli. Substitute regular baking powder in equal amounts.

Ammonium Carbonate

Called *ammoniaca* in Italian and sometimes known as hartshorn in English, ammonium carbonate is the secret to that crisp-but-not-crunchy texture in many *biscotti secchi*, or dry cookies. The gas produced by ammonium carbonate creates small, identical air cells, which give a lighter, more friable texture to baked goods; baking powder creates air cells of varying sizes, resulting in a more clunky texture. Unlike baking powder, which can leave a metallic taste, ammonium carbonate leaves no unpleasant aftertaste.

But beware: during baking your kitchen will smell *bad*. The first time I used ammonium carbonate, nobody had warned me. My kitchen smelled like cat pee. I threw the whole batch of biscotti away. I was sure I'd done something wrong, so I tried again. Cat pee again. I tossed that batch too. Then I learned that the smell goes away when the moisture is baked out and the gas is rendered inert. Not very appetizing, but I promise you it's worth it. Just don't take a deep breath when you open the oven.

Spices

SPEZIE

Cinnamon

Cinnamon is an entirely different story in Sicilian sweets. It's not that cozy autumnal flavor you get in apple pie or cinnamon buns or a pumpkin spiced latte. That's because, instead of vanilla, cinnamon is most often paired with lemon or mandarin zest in baked goods. Like a metaphor for Sicily itself, cinnamon's character becomes more assertive and complex, and even a bit mysterious. For an even deeper flavor, toast ground cinnamon in a dry skillet over medium heat, stirring until it releases its aroma. Cool completely before using.

Cloves

I can remember vividly, from when I was a small child, my great-grandmother's tiny silver box with its rose soldered onto the top. She kept it in her purse, filled with whole cloves that she chewed on when she needed a little pick-me-up or to freshen her breath. Like cinnamon, cloves take on a whole new character in Sicilian sweets. They're often combined with citrus or chocolate or candied fruit, and they lend a flavor that I can only describe as haunting, in the sense of having such great beauty as to be memorable. Whole cloves keep their flavor for months, while ground cloves lose their intensity quickly: best to buy only as much as you'll need at a time.

Fennel and Anise

One of my favorite things to do in early autumn, whether in Sicily or California, is to pluck the seeds from fennel plants that have flowered and dried on the side of the road. These seeds are smaller than those you'll find at the store, with a flavor that's more spicy than sweet. Obviously, cultivated fennel seeds are what you'll probably use; I suggest toasting these in a dry skillet over medium heat, stirring, until they release their fragrance. Cool them completely before using.

I use both anise seeds and star anise in this book: seeds in doughs and star anise in liquids. Buy the freshest you can find. Both keep their strength for several months.

Aromas and Essences

AROMI

Fiori di Sicilia

The flavoring extract *fiori di Sicilia*, or flowers of Sicily, isn't from Sicily at all, but it should be. Orange, vanilla, and floral essences combine to create a flavor that's warm, spicy, and smooth. It works almost anywhere you'd use pure vanilla extract. I love it so much I wear it as perfume. I've tried several brands, but the only one I can recommend is from King Arthur. Others have been downright horrible.

To make your own fiori di Sicilia, pour 2 cups (480 ml) of vodka into a jar and add the zest from 1 blood orange and 2 vanilla beans, split lengthwise. Put the lid on the jar and keep it in a cool, dark place for 40 days, shaking gently once or twice each day to distribute the flavors. Then stir in 1 tablespoon of orange-blossom water and 1 teaspoon of rose water, cover, and shake to mix. It gets better the longer it sits. Store in a cool, dark place for up to a year, and shake before using.

Vanilla

Most Sicilians use *vanillina*, little 3-gram packets of artificial vanilla powder, in their baking, and so do I, especially in biscotti. It's a flavor from my childhood, which probably has more to do with why I like it than its quality. By all means use a good-quality vanilla extract instead. Each packet of vanillina is equal to 1 teaspoon of vanilla extract.

Extracts

Almond, anise, orange flower, lemon, and orange extracts come in 2-gram vials in Sicily. One vial is equal to ½ teaspoon. I also use jasmine and bergamot extracts that I buy from an online source called OliveNation. Make sure you're buying flavor extracts and not oils.

Rose Water and Orange-Blossom Water

These are less potent than extracts, and are available at any Middle Eastern, Greek, or Indian market, or online.

Dried Fruits, Nuts, and Seeds

FRUTTA SECCA

Figs

There's nothing better than leaning out a window and plucking a fat, ripe fig fresh from the tree. If you're lucky enough to have access to a tree, dry some of the figs yourself, to use in baking.

First, split them all the way to (but not through) the stem, keeping both sides connected. Put them cut side up on a rack in the sun. The best place to do this is on the dashboard of a car, where the sun beats down and other living things can't get to them. Bring the figs indoors at night, unless you use the dashboard method. Depending on the strength of the sun, they can take two to three days to dry. Store them in a jar with dried bay leaves on the bottom.

If you're buying already-dried figs, look for Smyrna or Calimyrna figs. They're often softer, with a mild, honey-like flavor. Black Mission figs are good too. Look for fruits that are plump; too dry, and their natural sugars can become bitter.

Raisins

The absolute best raisins in Sicily are from Zibibbo grapes, which are grown on the island of Pantelleria and dried in the hot Sicilian sun. They're a burnished red color, with the perfect balance of sweetness and tartness. They're available online at Gustiamo.com. *Uva sultanina* are the most widely available and commonly used raisins in Sicily. They come from green grapes that are more sweet than tart, and range from golden to light brown in color. Red flame raisins are a good substitute, with Thompson seedless raisins a second. Golden raisins are too tart for the recipes in this book.

Nuts

Don't expect to find dried apricots and peaches when you see the words *frutta secca*, or dried fruit. In Sicily, this most often means nuts, which are indeed the fruits of their respective trees. **Almonds** are the most

beloved of these, and Sicilian sweets wouldn't be what they are without them. The tree (*mandorlo*) is considered masculine, while the fruit (*mandorla*) is feminine. The almond tree is a symbol of strength and virility, being the first tree to push through the winter and flower in the spring. (*Scusi*, but it doesn't take much to push through a temperate Sicilian winter.) Almonds' association with love and fidelity is perhaps stronger, and the tradition of sugared almonds at weddings goes back to ancient Rome, if not further. In the Old Testament, Samson courted Delilah with branches of almond blossoms. A very charming man once told me my eyes were the shape of Sicilian almonds. The best almonds are *pizzuta* from Avola, though all Sicilian almonds are flavorful and sweet.

A word on **bitter almonds**, which are called for in two recipes in this book, *marzapane* (page 62) and *latte di mandorla* (page 224). They are illegal in the U.S. because of their natural cyanide content. In Sicily, a ratio of 10 percent bitter almonds to 90 percent sweet almonds are used in sweets. But there is a workaround if you are in the U.S. In some Middle Eastern markets, you can find sweet apricot kernels, which can be substituted 1-to-1 for bitter almonds. The kernels, which are found inside the apricot pits, are mildly bitter and won't kill you even if you eat a handful. See the recipe headnote for latte di mandorla on page 224 for more about bitter-almond substitution.

In Sicily, **hazelnuts** are grown in the area around Mount Etna and in the Nebrodi and Madonie mountains, though I'm not alone in thinking that the hazelnuts from Piemonte in Northern Italy are better.

Many Sicilian **pistachios** are grown in the province of Agrigento, but by far the best ones are Bronte pistachios, grown in volcanic soil at the base of Mount Etna in the town of Bronte.

Sesame Seeds

I buy sesame seeds from Middle Eastern markets. They tend to go rancid quickly, so buy them in small amounts or keep them in the freezer. Toast them in a dry skillet over medium heat, stirring, to bring out their flavor. Cool them completely before using.

◆◆◆

A OCCHIO

Baking by Eye

◆◆◆

My nonna measured everything with the tip of her finger or a teacup. She had *mani sapienti*, or knowledgeable hands. *Mani* don't become *sapienti* overnight, or by watching a few YouTube videos, or taking a 3-hour class or a food tour to a picturesque Sicilian town. You must develop a feel for your ingredients, the weight of your own hand full of flour or of a lump of biscotti dough, the size of the bubbles in a *crema pasticcera*, the sound of a hissing coffee pot, or the scent of a cake when it's ready to come out of the oven.

Some Sicilians love gadgets (the multipurpose Bimbi, which takes up as much counterspace as a small truck, is a current favorite), while others make do with little more than a plastic-handled knife and a wooden board and maybe, but not always, a scale. Your hand is your most efficient tool and your own unit of measure. A *manciata* is a handful, and a *pugno* is a fistful (the *pugnietta* is smaller). Two finger-widths is just the right amount of space between portions of cookie dough on a baking sheet, while the bit of your pinkie finger from the last knuckle to the tip is enough baking powder to leaven a cup of flour. *Un pizzico qua, un pizzico là* means "a little pinch here, a little pinch there." Speaking of pinches, and this is only an observation: a Sicilian pinch is typically done with five fingers, whereas an American pinch is two.

How much of any given ingredient will you need? *Quanto basta,* or q.b. for short, which means "as much as is needed." As much as is needed for *what*? For it to be right. But if you ask a Sicilian how much, exactly? *Ah non molto*, not too much, or *a occhio,* to the eye. The question of when it is right can only be answered by developing mani sapienti.

Let's say you're heating oil to fry *arancine*. Forget the thermometer. Instead, dip the end of a wooden spoon in the oil, touching the bottom of the pot. If bubbles immediately form around it, the oil's ready.

Then there's the old *prova della carta,* to test the heat of an oven. Put a piece of untreated white paper in the oven. If it turns chestnut brown in 5 minutes, the oven is at the right temperature to bake biscotti. If it languishes at *bionda,* or blond, put more wood on the fire, and if it burns, take some out.

I learned from my nonna that properly risen bread dough should feel like my earlobe (which, coincidentally, feels like properly risen bread dough).

Why is it important to learn to bake intuitively? It isn't really, but over time, baking this way becomes like a meditation practice that helps to develop an inner sense of balance. Your body learns its own rhythm and physical wisdom; your hands become more sensitive and surer. Learning to listen and feel and hear and smell your baking more actively keeps you operating in the right now and helps you to trust your own judgment. Before long, you'll develop those mani sapienti—and this wisdom is the sort that has benefits far beyond the kitchen.

◆◆◆

BRONTE PISTACHIOS

PISTACCHI DI BRONTE

Imagine a landscape of black lava boulders as far as the eye can see, dipping into valleys and up hills, at the foot of an active volcano. Now picture dozens upon dozens of gnarled pistachio trees, some as old as 150 years, pushing through and emerging from the boulders, wherever they can find space. This is I Lochi, a very old, very special pistachio grove in Bronte, and we were there to join in the harvest.

Bronte pistachios are the most prized in Sicily, and I Lochi is one of only three pistachio growers in Sicily included in the Slow Food Presidia, an organization that protects traditional foods, traditional methods of growing or processing them, and rural landscapes or ecosystems at risk of extinction.

Ten years ago, Luigi Paladino left his veterinary practice to take over the family pistachio operation from his grandfather. (He tells us his parents wanted nothing to do with it, having recently retired from careers in banking.) Together with his business partner, Biagio Schillirò, he oversees 20 hectares of those gnarled pistachio trees, growing, harvesting, drying, and shelling them in the traditional way—all by hand, one by one, in the blistering Sicilian sun.

Unlike other farms where trees are planted on level ground in neat rows, these trees grow spontaneously—they are not planted, but spring up from the mineral-rich lava rocks when Mother Earth wills, wherever she wills. They are not pollinated by the farmers—pollen is carried naturally on the April winds from male to female trees. By May, fruit begins to form on the female trees, and by late September, when the fruit turns from red to white, they are ready for harvest.

Because the terrain is so rough and machines cannot navigate the steep hills and deep valleys of lava rock where they grow, it must all be done by hand. Forty men, with canvas sacks strapped across their bodies, harvest each pistachio—by hand, and on foot—in two weeks.

Pistachio trees bear fruit only in odd-numbered years. During the off years, any small fruit that may appear is plucked off by hand to allow the nutrients to return to the tree. Once harvested, the *mallo*, or soft outer husks, are removed (these purportedly have anti-aging properties and are made into facial creams), the pistachios are shelled, and then laid out in the sun, where they will dry for three days before being packed for sale. The cycle is completed during winter, when the pistachio shells are taken out into the fields and burned, carrying nutrients to the trees on the winds of Mother Nature.

Pizzuta almonds, Bronte pistachios, and Piedmontese hazelnuts are all sold on **Gustiamo.com**, my favorite Italian importer. Piedmontese hazelnuts are readily available online. Look for "premium IGP hazelnuts." The IGP designation (Indicazione Geografica Protetta, or Protected Geographical Indication) means that a product is closely linked to a geographic area.

MORNING *Cookies*

BISCOTTI DEL MATTINO

milk biscuits

BISCOTTI AL LATTE

Makes 20

Sicilians—in fact Italians in general—love cookies for breakfast (also cake and ice cream, but we'll get to that later). Morning cookies aren't overly sweet, but are simple, dry, dunkable biscuits that slurp up milky coffee at the start of a day. I didn't grow up with these, but they've become my favorite. Ammonium carbonate (see page 22) gives them a satisfying crunch that's almost as pleasant to the ear as it is to the mouth. No other leavening will give you the same texture, but baking powder will come close. Don't let the smell scare you: the ammonium that you smell turns to gas and evaporates in the baking process.

½ cup (100 g) sugar, plus ⅓ cup (70 g) for decorating

2 eggs

3½ tablespoons (50 ml) canola oil

3½ tablespoons (50 ml) milk

2 teaspoons ammonium carbonate, or 2 teaspoons baking powder

1 teaspoon vanilla extract

2¾ cups (330 g) all-purpose flour, or 2½ cups (300 g) 00 flour

Preheat the oven to 350°F (180°C). Line two baking sheets with parchment paper. Place ⅓ cup (70 g) of the sugar on a large plate.

In a large bowl, whisk together the remaining ½ cup (100 g) sugar and the eggs with a wire whisk. Then whisk in the oil and the milk, and finally the ammonium and vanilla. Switch to a wooden spoon and stir in half the flour until the batter is smooth. Add the rest of the flour one big spoonful at a time, mixing well as you go, until you have a nice smooth dough that—if you've used the ammonium carbonate (as you absolutely should)—will smell like pee. Open a window and hold your nose; it'll be worth it.

Turn the dough out onto a lightly floured surface and knead gently a few times, then divide it into half. Divide each half into 10 pieces. Roll each piece into a log about 1 inch (2.5 cm) wide and 4 inches (10 cm) long, then roll the log in the plate of sugar until it's completely coated; then transfer to one of the baking sheets. Continue with the rest of the dough, placing the logs about two finger-widths apart on the baking sheets.

Bake for 20 to 25 minutes, or until nicely browned. Cool completely on a wire rack, then store airtight for up to a week.

breakfast braids

TRECCINE

◆◆◆

Makes
32

◆◆◆

My grandmother and her grandmothers before her produced a steady supply of these cookies throughout their adult lives. On top of her fridge, Nonna kept a tin of them, and we dunked them in coffee, milk, and the tears of life's little disappointments. A thread of superstition and symbolism runs through Sicilian life: *treccine* (braids)—of which there are many in Sicilian pastry—are a symbol of unity and strength. They also symbolize protection against evil, another thing Sicilians are somewhat preoccupied with.

3⅓ cups (400 g) all-purpose flour, or 3 cups (360 g) 00 flour

2 teaspoons baking powder

½ teaspoon fine sea salt

¾ cup (150 g) sugar

⅔ cup (160 ml) canola oil

4 eggs

Grated zest of half a lemon

Grated zest of half an orange

¼ cup (35 g) sesame seeds or pistachio flour (optional)

Preheat the oven to 375°F (190°C). Line two baking sheets with parchment paper.

Sift together the flour, baking powder, and salt and set aside. In a large bowl, whisk together the sugar and oil with a wire whisk.

In a separate bowl, beat the eggs with a fork to combine. Transfer 2 tablespoonfuls of the egg to a small bowl and set aside. Whisk the remaining eggs into the sugar and oil mixture.

Switch to a wooden spoon and stir the lemon and orange zests into the egg mixture, then add the flour mixture in large spoonfuls, stirring as you go.

Turn the dough out onto a lightly floured surface and knead gently a few times. Divide the dough into 4 pieces, then divide each piece into 8. Roll each piece of dough into an 8-inch (20 cm) rope, then fold each rope in half, joining the two ends and twisting a few times to form a two-strand treccina, or braid. As you form them, place the braids two finger-widths apart on the baking sheets. When the braids are all formed, brush them with the reserved egg and sprinkle with the sesame seeds or pistachio flour.

Bake for 15 to 20 minutes, or until nicely browned. Remove from the oven and cool completely, then store airtight for up to 1 week.

anisette toasts

BISCOTTI ALL'ANICE

◆◆◆

Makes 24

◆◆◆

When I was a kid, I used to think Stella D'oro was a friend of my grandmother's. Every so often, Nonna would produce a jar full of dunking cookies that had the texture of toast, an inelegant amount of anise extract, and perhaps too much sugar—but I loved them. She'd say they were from Stella D'oro, but it never occurred to me that Nonna would feed me something *store-bought*. (I did wonder why she used Stella's last name if they were friends.) Not until I saw the package at a friend's house did I discover the truth. Here is my re-creation of those toasts, with a little less sugar and just enough anise.

2¼ cups (270 g) all-purpose flour, or 2 cups (240 g) 00 flour

2 teaspoons baking powder

3 eggs

⅔ cup (135 g) sugar

⅓ cup (80 ml) canola oil

2 teaspoons anise extract

½ teaspoon fiori di Sicilia (see page 23) or vanilla extract

½ teaspoon fine sea salt

Grated zest of half a lemon

Preheat the oven to 350°F (180°C). Line two baking sheets with parchment paper.

Sift together the flour and the baking powder and set aside.

In the bowl of a stand mixer with the whisk attachment, whip the eggs with the sugar until light and thickened, about 5 minutes. With the mixer running, add the oil a little at a time. Then add the anise extract, fiori di Sicilia, salt, and lemon zest. Turn the mixer to the lowest speed and add the flour mixture gradually, blending until the dough is smooth.

Spoon half of the dough along the center of one of the baking sheets, making a rectangle that's about 14 inches (35 cm) long and 3 inches (7.5 cm) wide. Using a spatula, neaten up the rectangle's edges a bit so it bakes evenly. Repeat with the rest of the dough on the other baking sheet.

Bake for 15 to 18 minutes, until the top springs back when you touch it lightly and it's just beginning to brown. The dough will have spread quite a bit. Remove the baking sheets from the oven and turn the oven down to 300°F (150°C). Cool the baked rectangles on the baking sheets for 10 minutes, then transfer them to a cutting board. With a sharp knife, slice each rectangle crosswise into strips 1 inch (2.5 cm) wide and lay them cut side down on the baking sheets.

Bake for 10 minutes, flip the biscotti over, and bake for another 10 minutes. They should be light brown on both sides. Transfer to a wire rack to cool completely, then store airtight for up to 2 weeks.

queen's biscuits

REGINELLE

Makes 24

Every Sicilian bakery in every city I've visited makes these cookies—perhaps because they're simple and dependable and they travel well. The queen for whom they're named is Queen Margherita of Savoy—the first queen of the newly unified Italy and the same Margherita for whom the pizza is named.

Most of the recipes in this book are butter- or olive oil-based, but I implore you to try using lard—or at least half lard and half butter—in these. I also recommend ammonium carbonate, the ancient leavener sometimes called hartshorn, which is available in Italian, German, and Scandinavian markets or by mail order. The *reginelle* will be crisp but crumbly, with no trace of the metallic taste you can get from baking powder. If you can find it, use flowery, citrusy *fiori di Sicilia* (see page 23); vanilla extract is a fine substitute.

2 eggs

¾ cup (110 g) sesame seeds, toasted (see page 25)

2¼ cups (270 g) all-purpose flour, or 2 cups (240 g) 00 flour

2 teaspoons ammonium carbonate, or 2 teaspoons baking powder

¾ cup (100 g) lard or unsalted butter or half butter and half lard, at room temperature

½ cup (100 g) sugar

¼ cup (60 ml) milk

½ teaspoon fiori di Sicilia (see page 23), or 1 teaspoon vanilla extract

½ teaspoon fine sea salt

Preheat the oven to 350°F (180°C). Line two baking sheets with parchment paper.

Separate the eggs, placing the whites and yolks in separate bowls. Place the toasted sesame seeds on a large plate. Sift the flour and ammonium carbonate into a medium bowl and set aside.

In a large bowl, stir together the lard and sugar, mixing well to combine. Add the egg yolks and milk, stirring as you go. Stir in the fiori di Sicilia and salt and mix well. Finally, add the flour mixture and stir until you have a smooth dough. Turn it out onto a lightly floured board and knead it gently a few times.

Divide the dough into fourths, then divide each fourth into 6 pieces. Roll each piece into a 12- by ½-inch (30 by 1.3 cm) log. Cut each log into four 3-inch (7.5 cm) pieces. Dip each piece into the egg whites, then roll it in the sesame seeds. Place the dough pieces two finger-widths apart on the baking sheets.

Bake for 25 to 30 minutes, until firm and nicely browned. (During this time your kitchen will smell like cat pee if you've used the ammonium carbonate—and I hope you will. Fear not, the smell *will* disappear and it *will* be worth it. Just open a window and hold your nose in the meantime.) Let the reginelle cool completely, then store them airtight for up to a month.

"S" cookies

BISCOTTI A ESSE

◆◆◆

Makes 48

◆◆◆

No matter how many people I've asked, the answer to "How did these cookies get their shape?" is either a cheeky "From my hands" or "Because they're called 'S' cookies." What I want to know is, *why* are they shaped like an *S*? Is it a throwback to the Sicilian mathematician Archimedes and his Archimedean spiral? Was the first person to ever make them named Santuzza or Smeralda or Signora someone?

Here's what I've settled on (it is backed up by no solid evidence whatsoever, but it sounds plausible enough to me): Sicily was the site of the goddess Persephone's abduction into the underworld by Hades. Hades disguised himself as a serpent to avoid detection; thus *S* is for the serpent who abducted Persephone. I find this plausible because many Sicilian pastries are shaped in tribute to something or someone awful. Perhaps in a twisted but somehow logical way, by eating these cookies, you're ingesting a kind of homeopathic protection against evil.

4¾ cups (570 g) all-purpose flour, or 4¼ cups (500 g) 00 flour

2 teaspoons baking powder

½ teaspoon baking soda

½ teaspoon fine sea salt

¾ teaspoon cinnamon

¾ cup (150 g) unsalted butter, or half butter and half lard, at room temperature

¾ cup (150 g) sugar

2 eggs

Grated zest of 1 lemon

¼ cup (60 ml) lemon juice (from 2 lemons)

Preheat the oven to 350°F (180°C). Line two baking sheets with parchment paper.

In a medium bowl, sift together the flour, baking powder, baking soda, salt, and cinnamon, and set aside.

In a large bowl, combine the butter and sugar and beat to mix well. If you do this by hand with a wooden spoon you will develop *mani sapienti*, wise hands, but of course it can be done with an electric mixer too. Add the eggs one at a time, beating well after each addition. Stir in the lemon zest and lemon juice. Now stir in the flour mixture and mix until everything is completely incorporated into a soft dough.

Turn the dough out onto a lightly floured surface and knead gently a few times. Divide the dough into fourths and divide each fourth into 12 pieces. Roll each piece into a 5-inch (13 cm) log and twist to form an S shape. Place the S on the baking sheet and continue shaping the rest of the dough, leaving a thumb's width between each S.

Bake for 20 to 25 minutes, until nicely browned and firm. Cool completely, then store airtight for up to a week.

KEEPING *Cookies*

BISCOTTI DA RIPOSTO

lemon- and fennel-scented almond biscotti

QUARESIMALI

◆◆◆

Makes 32

◆◆◆

If you're Catholic, you are supposed to give up something for Lent, the forty days of austerity and reflection preceding Easter. Depriving yourself of something indulgent is a sort of purification ritual, a small sacrifice to God. Some popular choices are alcohol, caffeine, and gossip. You're meant to suffer, if just a little. These biscotti are called *quaresimali* after *Quaresima*, or Lent. They are a bit challenging to chew, containing no lard, butter, or oil to make them tender. Small sacrifice: a dip into a little glass of one of Sicily's sweet wines, such as Marsala, Malvasia, or Moscato di Noto, takes care of that.

2 eggs

¾ cup (150 g) sugar

Grated zest of 2 lemons

2 cups (200 g) almond flour

1 cup (120 g) all-purpose flour, or ¾ cup (100 g) 00 flour

1½ teaspoons baking powder

1 teaspoon fennel seeds

½ teaspoon fine sea salt

¾ cup (100 g) whole unsalted roasted almonds

Line two baking sheets with parchment paper.

In a large bowl, stir together the eggs, sugar, and lemon zest. Stir in the almond flour, all-purpose flour, baking powder, fennel seeds, and salt, mixing with a wooden spoon until a rough dough forms. Turn the dough out onto a lightly floured surface and add the almonds. Knead gently but with authority until the almonds are well distributed throughout the dough.

Divide the dough in two and transfer one-half to one of the prepared baking sheets. Pat it into a rectangular "loaf" 14 inches (35 cm) long and 2 inches (5 cm) wide. Repeat with the remaining dough on the other baking sheet. Cover the pans with kitchen towels and set aside for 30 minutes to allow the dough to rise a bit. Meanwhile, preheat the oven to 325°F (160°C).

Bake for 25 to 30 minutes, or until the loaves are firm and nicely browned. Let cool completely, then wrap the whole loaves in kitchen towels and leave them at room temperature for 12 hours or overnight.

When you are ready for the second bake, unwrap the loaves and, with a sharp knife, slice them crosswise into strips ¾ inch (2 cm) wide. (Eat the ends as a cook's treat or give them to someone you love.) Place the quaresimali cut side down on the baking sheets and put the sheets into the cold oven.

Turn the oven on to 325°F (160°C) and bake for 20 minutes, then flip them over and bake for another 15 minutes, or until both sides are golden brown. Cool completely, then store in an airtight container. They will suffer attrition as they are eaten, but will last for as many of the 40 days of Lent as you allow.

spiced chocolate cookies

TETÙ E TEIO

◆◆◆

Makes 24

◆◆◆

November 1 is a major holiday in Sicily; it's Ognissanti, or All Saints' Day. The next day, November 2, is All Souls' Day, which is devoted to honoring relatives who have passed away. Somber though that may sound, it's a rather festive day, with visits to graveyards to pay tribute to deceased relatives with flowers, candles, and food. Children receive baskets—purportedly left for them by said relatives—with toys, sweet treats, and *pupi di zucchero*, or sugar puppets. These cookies always find their way into those baskets, along with a lemon version (sometimes called *teio al limone* or *taralli al limone*; see page 48) and hand-painted *frutta martorana* (see page 58). The cookies' name, *tetù e teio,* comes from Sicilian dialect for *tieni tu e tengo io,* or "one for you and one for me."

1½ cups (360 g) unsalted butter, at room temperature

1⅓ cups (270 g) sugar

2 eggs

1½ cups (150 g) almond flour

½ cup (120 ml) milk

2 teaspoons vanilla extract

1 teaspoon fine sea salt

4 cups (480 g) all-purpose flour, or 3½ cups (420 g) 00 flour

½ cup (45 g) unsweetened cocoa

1 tablespoon baking powder

1½ teaspoons ground cloves

1 teaspoon ground cinnamon

Glaze

1 cup (115 g) powdered sugar

1 teaspoon unsweetened cocoa

2 to 3 tablespoons boiling water

Line two baking sheets with parchment paper. Have a large cooling rack ready.

In a large bowl, stir together the butter and sugar, combining well. Add the eggs one at a time, stirring well as you go. Then stir in the almond flour, milk, vanilla, and salt.

In another bowl, sift together the all-purpose flour, cocoa, baking powder, cloves, and cinnamon, and add this to the first mixture, stirring well until evenly incorporated. Don't overmix. Cover and chill for 30 minutes.

Preheat the oven to 350°F (180°C).

Scoop spoonfuls of the dough and roll into balls in the palms of your hands. Place the balls two finger-widths apart on the baking sheets. Bake for 15 to 18 minutes, until the tops are set when touched lightly with your finger. The centers should still be a bit soft.

Meanwhile, make the glaze. Sift the powdered sugar and cocoa together into a small bowl. Whisk in the boiling water until smooth.

When the tetù are baked, let them cool for 10 minutes, then dip the top of each one into the glaze and transfer, icing side up, to the cooling rack and let cool completely. Store airtight in the fridge for up to a week. Bring the cookies to room temperature before serving.

At left, Chef Giuseppe Sciurcia, hand painting traditional *pupi di zucchero*, or sugar puppets for All Souls' Day.

iced lemon rings

TARALLI AL LIMONE

Makes 24

When made in the shape of angels' halos, these soft lemon-glazed cookies are called *taralli*. The same cookies in other shapes are called *tetù al limone* and *anginetti*, or lemon drops in Italian American bakeries. Along with chocolate *tetù e teio* and the painted sugar puppets called pupi di zucchero, taralli are given to children on All Souls' Day, purportedly by dearly departed relatives.

¾ cup (150 g) unsalted butter, at room temperature

⅔ cup (135 g) sugar

2 eggs

½ cup (120 ml) milk

1 teaspoon vanilla extract

Grated zest and juice of 2 lemons

1 teaspoon fine sea salt

4¾ cups (570 g) all-purpose flour, or 4¼ cups (500 g) 00 flour

1 teaspoon baking powder

1 teaspoon baking soda

Glaze

2 cups (230 g) powdered sugar

1 tablespoon unsalted butter, melted

3 to 4 tablespoons (45 to 60 ml) lemon juice (from 1 lemon)

Line two baking sheets with parchment paper. Have a large cooling rack ready.

In a large bowl, stir together the butter and sugar, combining well. Add the eggs one at a time, stirring well as you go. Then stir in the milk, vanilla, zest and juice, and salt.

In another bowl, sift together the flour, baking powder, and baking soda and add this to the first mixture, stirring well until evenly incorporated: don't overmix. Cover and chill for 1 hour.

Preheat the oven to 350°F (180°C).

Turn the dough out onto a lightly floured surface and divide it into fourths. Divide each fourth into six. Roll each piece of dough into a 12-inch (30 cm) rope. Fold in half side by side to make a 6-inch (15 cm) double-strand rope. Twist together, then form the twisted rope into a circle, press the ends together, and place on a baking sheet. Form the rest of the dough ropes into circles and place them two finger-widths apart on the baking sheets.

Bake for 15 to 18 minutes, until bionda—blond—or ever-so-slightly browned.

Meanwhile, make the glaze. Sift the powdered sugar into a medium bowl. Whisk in the melted butter and the lemon juice until smooth.

When the taralli are baked, let them cool for 5 minutes, then carefully dip the tops of each one into the glaze and transfer, icing side up, to the cooling rack to cool completely. Store airtight in the fridge for up to a week. Bring the cookies to room temperature before serving.

soft cookie clouds

NUVOLETTE

◆◆◆

Makes 20

◆◆◆

These puffy, soft cookies are a minor miracle, and miracles have a special place in the hearts of Sicilians. With only eggs, sugar, and flour, an ethereal pouf of a cookie results. Its texture is somewhere between a soft cookie and a cake, and light enough that you can easily eat too many.

It's said *nuvolette* were first made in a town in Sicily's interior called Monte Erei, by a World War II widow who had fallen on hard times. She used what few ingredients were available to her to make cookies—which proved so popular, they became a bit of a cottage industry. In San Cataldo, where some of the best ones are made, nuvolette are given to widows after Easter Mass, in remembrance of their husbands, the fallen soldiers.

One caveat: these aren't dunkers. They soften and disintegrate almost immediately when they hit liquid.

3 eggs

1⅓ cups (270 g) sugar

½ teaspoon fiori di Sicilia (see page 23), or 1 teaspoon vanilla extract

½ teaspoon fine sea salt

2¼ cups (270 g) sifted all-purpose flour, or 2 cups (250 g) sifted 00 flour

Preheat the oven to 375°F (190°C). Line two baking sheets with parchment paper.

In the bowl of a stand mixer with the whisk attachment, whip the eggs, sugar, fiori di Sicilia, and salt until light, fluffy, and tripled in volume, about 8 minutes. Switching to a large metal spoon, gently fold in the flour, a spoonful at a time, until all of it is incorporated.

Using the same large spoon, scoop up a large spoonful of the batter and turn it over onto one of the baking sheets, dragging the spoon along the pan to form the batter into a 3-inch (7.5 cm) log. Don't worry about making the nuvolette precise; the beauty of clouds is that they come in all shapes. Continue with the rest of the batter, leaving two finger-widths between each nuvoletta.

Bake for about 8 minutes, or until puffed and golden. Let cool for a few minutes, then remove to a rack to cool completely. Store airtight for up to a week.

spiced mosto cotto cookies

SPICCHITEDDI

♦♦♦

Makes 24

♦♦♦

Take the ferry from Milazzo, and the first of the Aeolian Islands you'll reach is Lipari. It's also the largest and the most populated island, and the one from which a number of very good—and very symbolic—pastries come.

Spicchiteddi are soft, not too sweet, and fragrant with warm spices, black pepper, and *mosto cotto*, or grape-must syrup (page 225). Although everyone has a different way of forming them, they always have spirals and exactly two whole blanched almonds per cookie. It is said that they ward against the *malocchio*, or evil eye, like so many things in Sicily do. Could be. The *moustokouloura* of Greece is a nearly identical recipe, also made with mosto cotto. Could this again be the work of Archimedes and his spirals? Or are they fashioned after the Norse *triskele* and brought down with the Normans in the tenth century? In whichever way they got here, they are soft, spicy, and delicious. If you don't happen to have mosto cotto at hand, Middle Eastern grape syrup or Greek *petimezi* make a fine substitute and are readily available in international markets.

4¼ cups (500 g) all-purpose flour, or 3¾ cups (450 g) 00 flour

2 teaspoons cinnamon

1 teaspoon ground cloves

1 teaspoon cardamom

1 teaspoon black pepper

1 teaspoon fine sea salt

1 teaspoon baking soda

1½ teaspoons baking powder

1 cup (240 ml) mosto cotto (page 225), or Middle Eastern grape syrup

¼ cup (60 g) unsalted butter, melted

1 sachet vanillina (see page 23), or 1 teaspoon vanilla extract

Zest of 2 mandarins and 1 lemon, or 1 orange and 1 lemon

1 cup (120 g) whole blanched almonds

Line two baking sheets with parchment paper.

Sift together the flour, cinnamon, cloves, cardamom, pepper, salt, baking soda, and baking powder into a large bowl.

In a small bowl, whisk together the mosto cotto, melted butter, vanillina, and zest. Stir this into the flour mixture, mixing well to combine and form a dough. Cover and chill for 1 hour.

Preheat the oven to 350°F (180°C).

Turn the dough out onto a lightly floured surface and divide it into fourths. Divide each fourth into 12 pieces. Roll the pieces into ropes about 4 inches (10 cm) long and curl them into spirals of different sizes and shapes. As you work, place the spirals on the baking sheets with two finger-widths between each. Push the spirals together in pairs. When they are all formed, press 2 almonds into each cookie.

Bake for 15 to 20 minutes, until firm to the touch and nicely browned. Allow to cool completely, then store airtight for up to a month.

fig and olive shortbreads

FROLLINI AI FICHI E OLIVE

◆◆◆

Makes 24 to 30

◆◆◆

Olives are fruits, so why not treat them as such? A good salt-cured ripe black olive that's been stored in oil has the texture of a plump raisin, and a similar sort of concentrated flavor. When my auntie Connie moved from Sicily to Northern California, she would pick perfectly good ripe olives that nobody wanted off city trees, take them home, put them in a cotton pillowcase full of salt, and hang it from a tree. Every day, she shook the pillowcase, and the olives' bitter juices would seep through, staining the cotton. When the juices no longer flowed, the olives were done. After several rinses and a quick blanch in boiling water, they were dried and put *sott'olio*, or under oil.

To me, they were like raisins; and that's what gave me the idea of using them in a cookie. My first batch was unspectacular, but the idea was clearly worth pursuing. I added figs, and then toasted fennel seeds—all these ingredients grow in Sicily and play well together in other contexts, so why not here?

As I'm writing this, I wonder what the reaction in Sicily will be to olives in a cookie. (I think I know.) Nevertheless, here I go, because it makes complete sense to me; and it will to you too, once you taste these sweet-savory shortbreads. I keep rolls of the unbaked dough in my freezer, to slice and bake whenever I need them.

The final version of the cookies has a very special mix of sweet, salty, buttery, crunchy, chewy, and earthy. Taste for yourself.

2 teaspoons fennel seeds

1 cup (230 g) unsalted butter, at room temperature

½ cup plus 1 tablespoon (115 g) sugar

1¾ cups (210 g) all-purpose flour, or 1½ cups (180 g) 00 flour

1 cup plus 2 tablespoons (130 g) almond flour

⅓ cup (100 g, or about 10) pitted and chopped oil-cured olives

2 fat, dried Calimyrna or Smyrna figs, or 3 dried black Mission figs, tops trimmed, and chopped

First, toast the fennel seeds. Place the seeds in a small dry skillet over medium-high heat. Toast, stirring, until they become darkened and fragrant, 3 to 4 minutes. Scrape the seeds onto a small plate and let them cool completely. Crush the seeds a bit with a heavy rolling pin or in a mortar and pestle—or, if you prefer, keep them whole.

In a large bowl, stir together the butter and sugar until well combined. Stir in the all-purpose flour and the almond flour and mix until a soft dough forms. Then stir in the fennel seeds, olives, and figs.

Turn the dough out onto a lightly floured surface and knead it gently a few times. Divide into to fourths and shape each fourth into an 8-inch (20 cm) log. Wrap the logs in parchment paper and refrigerate for at least 3 hours, and up to 12 hours.

Preheat the oven to 350°F (180°C). Line two baking sheets with parchment paper.

Unwrap the dough and slice crosswise into ¾-inch (2 cm) rounds, placing them two finger-widths apart on the baking sheets. Bake for 20 to 25 minutes, until lightly browned around the edges. The centers will be soft, but the *frollini* will crisp up as they cool. Let them cool completely on the baking sheets, then store airtight for up to a month.

sun-dried tomato and anise shortbreads

FROLLINI AL POMODORI SECCHI E ANICE

◆◆◆

Makes 24 to 30

◆◆◆

If you weigh the main ingredients here by ounces, it's a simple formula that scales up or down in the same proportions: 8 ounces of butter plus 4 ounces of sugar plus 8 ounces of wheat flour plus 4 ounces of almond flour. Instead of almond flour, you could use rice flour or semolina flour, both of which give these *frollini* a pleasantly gritty, toothy texture. Here again, I'm treating sun-dried tomatoes like the fruit they are. The anise just takes it to another, more aromatic level. Keep a roll of the dough in your freezer to slice and bake whenever you like.

¾ cup (130 g) sun-dried tomatoes

1 cup (230 g) unsalted butter, at room temperature

½ cup plus 1 tablespoon (115 g) sugar

1¾ cups (210 g) all-purpose flour, or 1½ cups (180 g) 00 flour

1 cup plus 2 tablespoons (130 g) almond flour

1 tablespoon anise seeds

½ teaspoon fine sea salt

If the tomatoes aren't soft and pliable, place them in a bowl and cover them with boiling water. Soak them for 10 minutes, then drain and pat dry. Finely chop the tomatoes and set them aside.

In a large bowl, stir together the butter and sugar until well combined. Stir in the wheat and almond flours and mix until a soft dough forms. Now stir in the anise seeds, salt, and chopped tomatoes.

Turn the dough out onto a lightly floured surface and knead it gently a few times. Divide it into fourths and shape each fourth into an 8-inch (20 cm) log. Wrap the logs in baking parchment and refrigerate for at least 3 hours.

Preheat the oven to 350°F (180°C). Line two baking sheets with parchment paper.

Unwrap the dough and slice crosswise into ¾-inch (2 cm) rounds, placing them two finger-widths apart on the baking sheets.

Bake for 20 to 25 minutes, until lightly browned around the edges. The centers will be soft but will crisp up as they cool.

Let the frollini cool completely on the baking sheets, then store them airtight for up to a month.

hazelnut and orange meringues

CROCCANTINI AL NOCCIOLE E ARANCIA CANDITE

◆◆◆

Makes
24

◆◆◆

There used to be a place in Taormina called Bar St. Honoré where they made these crunchy, chewy, nutty meringue cookies. I remember them well, not only for their unusually substantial texture (for a meringue) but because they got me through a brittle period when I discovered that my Sicilian boyfriend had a wife.

Years later, I found my way to an elderly Sicilian couple on YouTube who bickered and baked. It was from them that I learned this rather unusual method for making exactly the *croccantini* I remember from the Bar St. Honoré. And Bruno is still married.

2 egg whites

½ teaspoon fine sea salt

¾ cup (150 g) sugar

1 cup (150 g) chopped toasted hazelnuts

¼ cup (40 g) chopped candied orange peel (page 210)

Preheat the oven to 300°F (150°C). Line two baking sheets with parchment paper.

In the bowl of a stand mixer, whip the egg whites and salt until stiff. Gently fold in the sugar, a third at a time. Fold in the hazelnuts.

Scrape every bit of this mixture into a large saucepan. Over medium-low heat, stir constantly but gently for 10 minutes. The mixture will darken slightly. Remove from the heat and fold in the orange peel.

Drop the mixture by heaping tablespoons onto the baking sheets, leaving two finger-widths between each one.

Bake for 20 to 25 minutes, until lightly but decidedly browned and firm. The croccantini will crisp as they cool. Cool completely on the pans, then store airtight for up to a month.

ALMOND &

PASTICCINI DI

PISTACHIO *Sweets*

MANDORLE E PISTACCHI

TROMPE L'OEIL MARZIPAN

FRUTTA MARTORANA

Fruits to Fool the Bishop.
Or the King.

Santa Venerina is the sort of place you pass through on your way to other places, which is what we were doing when we discovered a jewel of a pastry shop. The town is now more shabby than chic, but the architectural embellishments on her small, crumbling baroque structures make you think that she was once quite the looker. Among all this faded beauty is the Pasticceria Russo, a charming example of Sicilian Baroque interior design—and of handcrafted *frutta martorana*.

Frutta martorana is named for the Benedictine monastery Santa Maria dell'Ammiraglio, nicknamed La Martorana, which itself is named for the Palermitan nobles Goffredo and Eloisa Martorana, who founded and financed the monastery in 1194. There is a legend that a bishop—or perhaps it was the king—was to pay a visit to the monastery. Beautiful though the monastery was, the fruit trees in the cloister garden were barren. The clever nuns busied themselves creating life-like fruits made of marzipan and painted to fool the eye, which they hung from the trees' branches. Walking through the garden, the bishop—or it could have been the king—declared it a miracle that this was the only garden in all of Palermo whose trees bore fruit out of season!

He bit into an ersatz lemon, only to discover that it tasted not of lemon but of almond, and he declared it to be fit for a king, thus giving it the name *pasta reale*, or royal paste, as it is sometimes called today.

Frutta martorana is found throughout Sicily and ranges from handmade and hand-painted to machine-made and airbrushed. It's becoming rarer to find the handmade sort that we found at the Pasticceria Russo. The proprietress, Anna, who runs the shop with her brother Salvatore and her daughter, son-in law, and grandchildren, invited us into the laboratorio to watch Chef Davide at work. There, he hand-formed figs, cherries, loquats, donut peaches, apricots, mulberries, strawberries, half-peeled mandarins, lemons, and cactus pears with muscle memory developed from over thirty years at the craft. Each one was painted and left to air-dry for a day before being glazed with a gum-arabic solution. Then we watched him adhere miniscule sugar spikes to the cactus pears with tiny dabs of royal icing. It occurred to me that so many things involving pastry are called "royal" here in Sicily. Of course. They're fit for a king. Or perhaps a bishop?

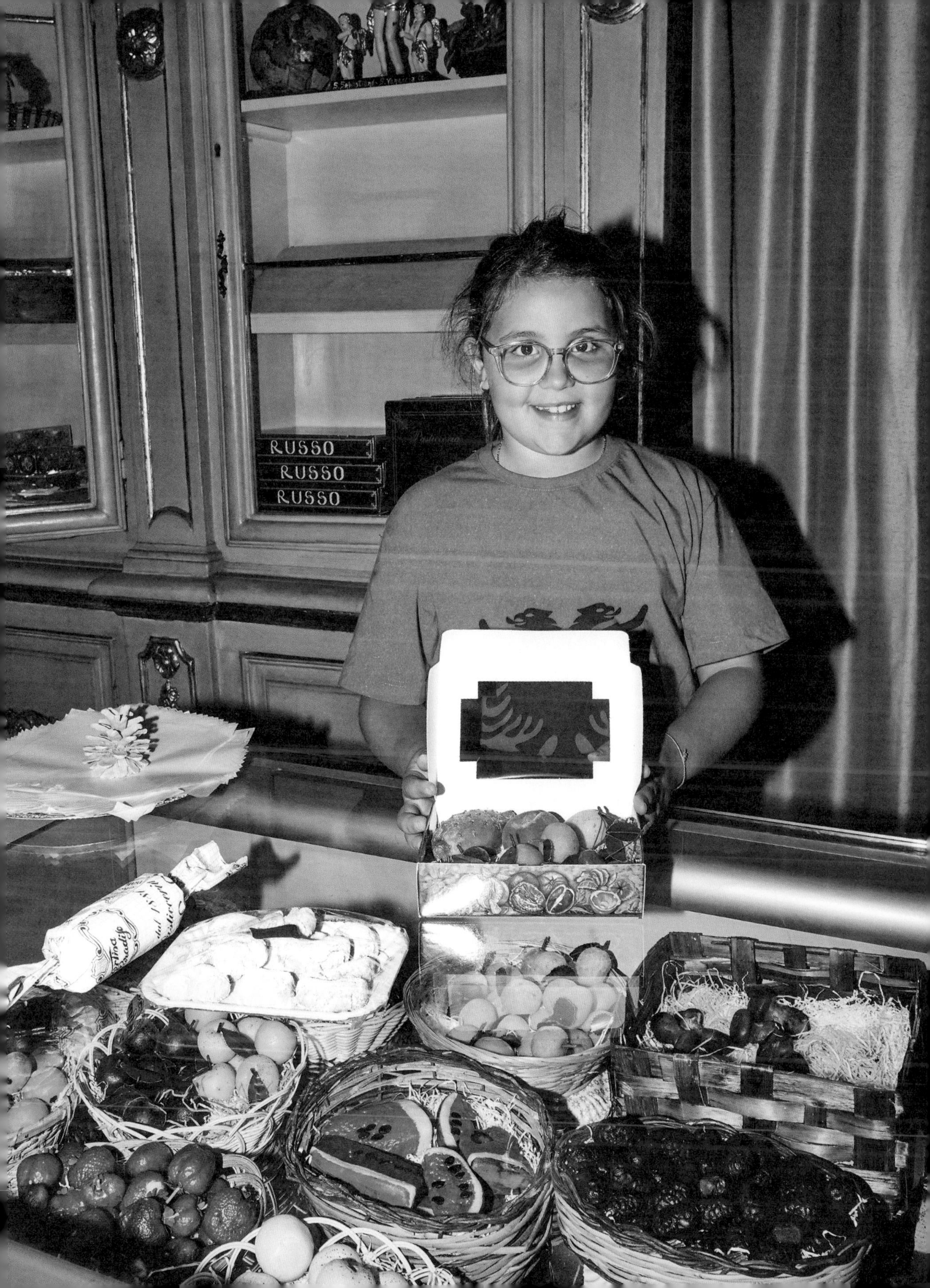
RUSSO
RUSSO
RUSSO

RUSSO
RUSSO
RUSSO
RUSSO

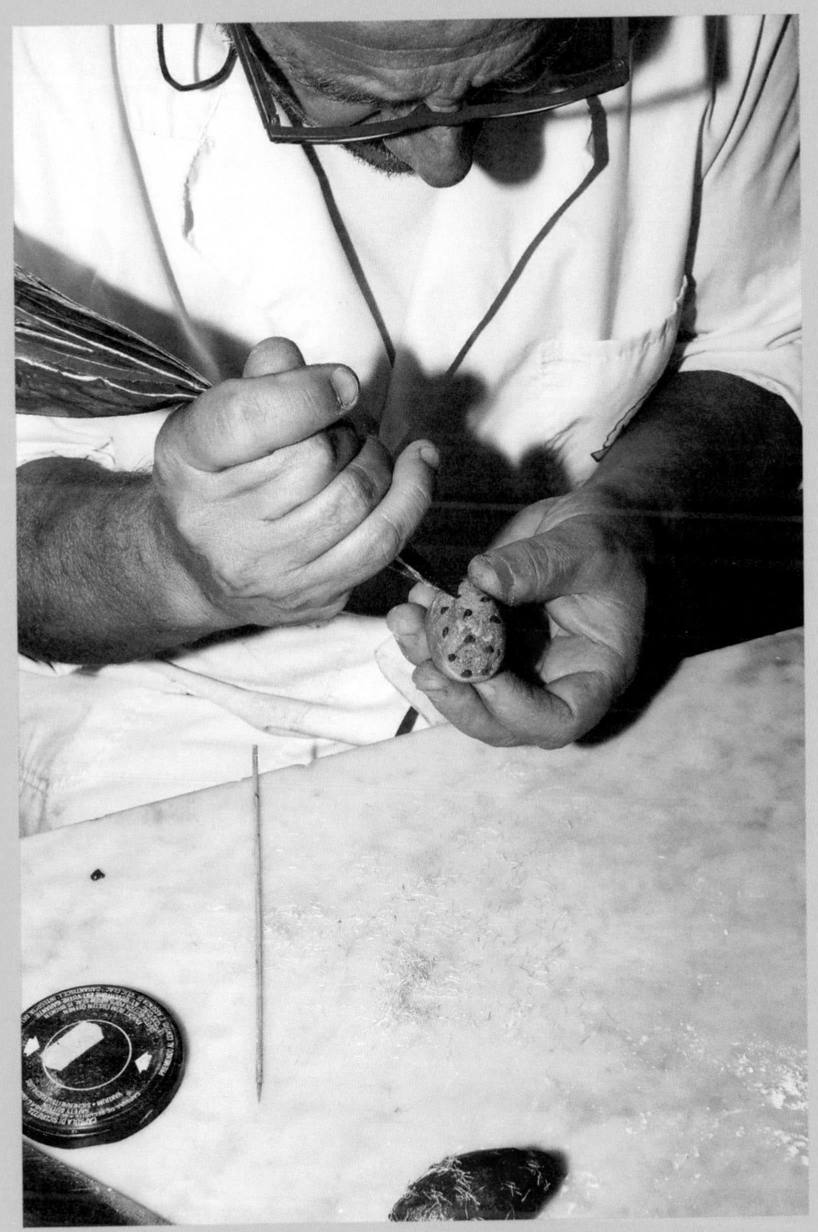

cooked marzipan

MARZAPANE O PASTA REALE

◆◆◆

Makes about 1½ pounds (680 g)

◆◆◆

I confess, I'm a fan of those little tubes of marzipan in the supermarket. The texture is compact and refined and well suited for sculpting *frutta martorana* (see page 58). It doesn't taste awful (it doesn't taste like anything), but homemade marzipan is worlds better and less costly. My grandfather dreamed endlessly about the marzipan he remembered from the Old Country, cut into diamond shapes and served at weddings. My nonna could tell you exactly how to make it, but she never once did. I don't have many regrets, but one is that I didn't try my hand at making cooked marzipan during my grandfather's lifetime. He would have loved it.

If you've never used bitter almonds or their alternative, apricot kernels, see page 224.

Seed oil, such as canola or sunflower, for the work surface

1⅔ cups (250 g) blanched almonds, or 2½ cups (250 g) almond flour

3 bitter almonds or apricot kernels, or ½ to 1 teaspoon almond extract

Grated zest of half a lemon

1¼ cups (250 g) granulated sugar

½ cup (120 ml) water

½ cup (120 ml) glucose syrup or corn syrup

2¼ cups (260 g) powdered sugar

Have ready a work surface or baking sheet rubbed with a bit of oil.

In a food processor with a steel blade, pulse the sweet almonds with the bitter almonds until finely ground. Add the lemon zest in the last few pulses. Transfer to a large bowl and set aside while you make the syrup.

Combine the granulated sugar, water and glucose or corn syrup in a small heavy-bottomed saucepan over medium-low heat; stir with a wooden spoon until the sugar is fully dissolved. Remove the spoon and don't put it back in until I tell you to. For now, just swirl the pan by its handle as the syrup cooks. Turn the heat up and boil until a candy thermometer inserted into the syrup registers 245°F (118°C). Remove the pan from the heat and immediately pour the syrup into the bowl containing the almond mixture. Stir with the wooden spoon until the mixture begins to cool and form a loose mass. Stir in the powdered sugar.

Turn the marzipan out onto the oiled work surface, rub your hands with a bit of oil, and knead the marzipan until it's nice and smooth and has fully cooled. At this point, you can form it into whatever shapes you like; or wrap it airtight and store it at room temperature until you're ready to use it, up to 2 weeks.

Pasta reale
Ingredienti : zucchero, mandorle, sciroppo di
aromi, acido sorbico (conservativo)
E110-E111-E122-

GELATERIA - ROSTICCERIA

I Segreti del Chiostro
Gli antichi dolci dei monasteri
PASTICCERIA
RUSSO
1880
SANTA VENERINA

almond blossoms

FIOR DI MANDORLA

◆◆◆

Makes 12

◆◆◆

This was the very first almond cookie I learned how to make. It was during the Clinton administration, and I found myself wandering around the back streets of Taormina searching for a coffee bar that didn't feature the word *turistico* in three languages on its signage. I finally found a little *pasticceria* painted bright red and with a faded picture of Bill Clinton in a frame above the pastry case. He had allegedly "just the other day" stopped in to buy their famous *fior di mandorla*, or almond blossoms: cookies that were soft on the inside, crispy on the outside, and dusted with powdered sugar. I had one or two or four with my coffee, then asked the owner how they were made.

His response was to invite me into the kitchen to see for myself. His son, a cheerful guy who had lost two fingers in an accident involving the electric almond grinder, asked if I would like to try my hand at grinding some almonds. In the electric almond grinder. No, *grazie mille*, I would not.

He made such a massive batch—by hand, and not measuring a thing—that there was no hope of my getting anything close to a recipe. What I did learn was to keep my hands out of the almond grinder, and that Bill Clinton had indeed just been in Taormina and may have been to their place and had their fior di mandorla. These are still my favorite little almond cookies, and nearly every pasticceria in Sicily makes them, sometimes calling them *fiocchi di neve*, or snowflakes.

½ cup (60 g) powdered sugar

2 egg whites

¼ teaspoon fine sea salt

¾ cup (150 g) granulated sugar

1 tablespoon honey

1 teaspoon vanilla extract

Grated zest of 1 lemon or 1 orange, or a little of each

2 cups (200 g) almond flour

Preheat the oven to 325°F (160°C). Line a baking sheet with parchment paper. Dust a work surface with the powdered sugar.

In a medium bowl, beat the egg whites and salt with an electric mixer until foamy and beginning to turn white. Add a spoonful of the granulated sugar and continue beating for a few seconds, then add the honey. Continue beating, adding the rest of the sugar in spoonfuls until stiff peaks form. Fold in the vanilla and the zest.

Now, gently but with authority, fold in the almond flour a third at a time, until the mixture comes together in a sticky dough. Turn the dough out onto the prepared work surface and roll it into a thick rope about 14 inches (35 cm) long. With a knife dipped in powdered sugar, cut the dough crosswise into 12 pieces. Place them on the baking sheet a finger-width apart, and pinch the centers a bit to form a squiggle. Dust with any remaining powdered sugar and bake for 12 to 15 minutes, until just barely beginning to take on color; they should be soft in the center. Cool the fior di mandorla completely and store airtight for up to a week.

almond cookies with sugared anise seeds or pine nuts

ANASINI O PIGNOLI AMARETTI

Makes 24

At the end of the caucus race, Alice (in Wonderland) reaches into her pocket to find a thimble and a box of comfits. Comfits, from Middle English *confyt* and Anglo-French *confit,* are seeds, nuts, or fruit in a hard confectionery coating. Jordan almonds are comfits, and *mukhwas,* the sugared seeds in a little bowl at the cash register in Indian restaurants, are comfits. Not so straightforward in Sicily, where paper confetti is called *coriandoli,* after the old tradition of throwing sugared coriander seeds at *carnevale,* weddings, and other happy occasions. What are sugared coriander seeds (and other comfits like Jordan almonds) called? *Confetti.*

These chewy almond cookies are coated in *anasini,* or anise comfits; the crunch of the sugar releases the herby licorice of the anise, then all of it gives way to the soft almond center—divine. Anasini aren't so easy to find outside of Italy. You could use Indian mukhwas, especially the fennel kind, instead—or pine nuts.

2 egg whites, plus another 2 for coating

1½ cups (210 g) pine nuts or 1 cup (150 g) anasini (sugared anise seeds)

¼ teaspoon fine sea salt

1 cup (200 g) sugar

½ teaspoon almond extract

2 cups (200 g) almond flour

Preheat the oven to 350°F (180°C). Line two baking sheets with parchment paper.

In a small, shallow bowl, whisk 2 of the egg whites with a fork until foamy. Set aside.

Place the pine nuts or anasini in another small bowl.

In a large bowl, beat the remaining 2 egg whites and the salt with an electric mixer until foamy and beginning to turn white. Add the sugar a spoonful at a time, continuing to beat, until all the sugar has been then the almond flour, gently but with authority, a third at a time.

Pinch off pieces of dough the size of a walnut and roll into balls; then roll in the egg whites in the shallow bowl and coat with the anisini or pine nuts. Place the *amaretti* on the baking sheets two finger-widths apart and, if you like, flatten them a bit with your fingers. Bake for 15 to 18 minutes, until golden brown. Cool completely, then store airtight for up to a week.

saint agatha's little olives

OLIVETTE DI SANT'AGATA

◆◆◆

Makes 24

◆◆◆

Another saint, more persecution, another miracle. Before there was Lucy, there was Agatha, born in Catania in the third century. Agatha, now patron saint of Catania, came across a barren olive tree while fleeing persecution under the Roman emperor Decius. It is said she touched the tree, which miraculously began to bear fruit, providing her both nourishment and refuge.

At the very baroque Pasticceria Russo in the province of Catania, *olivette di Sant'Agata* are made and presented with almost religious devotion, nestled in velvet in an antique pastry cupboard.

1¼ cups (250 g) sugar, plus ⅓ cup (60 g) for decorating

½ cup (120 ml) water

¼ teaspoon fine sea salt

2½ cups (250 g) almond flour

2 tablespoons *liquore alle erbe* (page 231), rum, or orange juice

Olive-green food coloring

Rub a baking sheet with a bit of canola or sunflower oil. Place the ⅓ cup (60 g) sugar for decorating in a small shallow bowl.

In a large heavy-bottomed saucepan over medium heat, combine the 1¼ cups (250 g) sugar with the water and salt, stirring with a wooden spoon until the sugar is fully dissolved. Add the almond flour a little at a time, stirring as you go, until all of it is incorporated. Lower the heat and cook, stirring continuously, until the mixture thickens and forms a dough that comes away from the sides and bottom of the pan. Stir in all of the liqueur and a few drops of the food coloring, mixing with the wooden spoon to distribute the color. Add more food coloring, a drop at a time, until the dough is the color of a green olive, or thereabouts.

Turn the dough out onto the baking sheet and set aside until cool enough to handle. Then transfer it to a lightly oiled work surface and knead it, gently but with authority, until smooth. Pinch off olive-sized pieces of dough and roll them with your hands into olive shapes. With a skewer, make an indentation in the larger end of each, where the stem would be. Roll each "olive" in the sugar in the small bowl, and place them on the baking sheet. Let dry, loosely covered with a cotton towel, for 24 hours, then store airtight for up to a week.

baked almond bonbons

PANINO DI SANTA CATERINA O MUCCUNETTI

◆◆◆

Makes 18

◆◆◆

So many monasteries claim these as their own that it's easy to see how they earned their place in the category of sweets known as *dolci da viaggio*, or sweets that travel. At the pastry shop I Segreti del Chiostro, housed in the former pastry kitchens of the Dominican monastery of Santa Caterina in Palermo, they are called *panino di Santa Caterina* and are simply dusted with powdered sugar. At the Benedictine monastery at Palma di Montechiaro, each one is wrapped in paper "*a caramella*," like fancy candies. At the Benedictine monastery of San Michele in Mazara del Vallo, they are coated in icing and called *muccunetti*. Did the nuns share recipes? Not likely. They were in cloistered convents, separated from the outside world. Recipes in convent kitchens were closely guarded and seldom recorded. What's most likely is that noble patrons traveled to other regions, bringing with them these traveling sweets, along with bragging rights to the monasteries—and the pastry kitchens—that they endowed.

½ cup (170 g) candied watermelon rind (page 215) or blood orange marmalade (page 196)

2 cups (200 g) finely ground almond flour

1¼ cups (150 g) powdered sugar

½ teaspoon cinnamon

¼ teaspoon fine sea salt

Grated zest of 1 lemon

1 tablespoon honey

1 egg white

Icing

⅓ cup (35 g) powdered sugar

1 tablespoon lemon juice or boiling-hot water

Line two baking sheets with parchment paper. Have ready a bowl of cold water for your hands.

Chop the watermelon rind or marmalade so finely that it forms a paste. Place in a small bowl and reserve.

In a large bowl, stir together the almond flour, powdered sugar, cinnamon, and salt.

In a small bowl, whisk together the lemon zest, honey, and egg white just enough to blend. Add this to the almond mixture and mix well until a soft dough is formed.

Wet your hands and pinch off a nut-sized piece of dough. In the palm of your hand, flatten the dough as thin as you can. Place a small spoonful of the preserves in the center and gather the dough around to enclose it. Pinch it closed and roll it until smooth, then transfer it to the baking sheet. Continue with the rest of the dough and preserves, leaving two finger-widths between each one. Let the muccunetti rest, uncovered, at room temperature for 4 hours.

Preheat the oven to 375°F (190°C). Bake for 10 minutes, or until very lightly browned. Let cool completely.

Meanwhile, make the icing. In a small bowl, whisk together the powdered sugar and the hot water or lemon juice until smooth. Cut waxed paper or parchment into eighteen 4-inch (10 cm) squares. When the muccunetti are cool, dip the tops in the glaze and return to the baking sheet to dry for 30 to 45 minutes. Then *chiudi a caramelle*—wrap each one in a square of paper, twisting the ends. Store airtight for up to a week.

the leopard's almond cookies

BISCOTTI RICCI DEL GATTOPARDO

◆◆◆

Makes
18 to 24

◆◆◆

In Giuseppe Tomasi di Lampedusa's semiautobiographical book *The Leopard*, the prince of Salina pays a visit to the Santo Spirito Monastery in Donnafugata to offer his customary benefaction. In that period, monasteries were typically founded and funded by aristocratic families who in turn purchased sweets from the nuns. Lampedusa writes, "The Prince liked the almond cakes the nuns made from an ancient recipe." At the Benedictine monastery in Palma di Montechiaro, where Lampedusa's country estate was located, cloistered nuns still make these cakes, just the way the Prince liked them. Orders are placed and received on the ancient foundling wheel, where infants were once abandoned to the care of the nuns.

5 cups (500 g) almond or pistachio flour, or a combination

1¾ cups (350 g) sugar, plus ¼ cup (50 g) for sprinkling

Grated zest of 1 lemon

½ teaspoon almond extract

½ teaspoon fine sea salt

3 eggs

Preheat the oven to 375°F (190°C). Line two baking sheets with parchment paper.

In a large bowl, combine the almond flour, 1¾ cups (350 g) of sugar, lemon zest, almond extract, salt, and eggs, and stir with a wooden spoon until the mixture comes together in a sticky dough.

Fit a cloth pastry bag with a ¾-inch (2 cm) star tip, or use a cookie press with the star disk. Fill with some of the dough and squeeze it onto the baking sheets in 6-inch (15 cm) lengths, forming each one into a loose S shape. Leave a thumb-width between each one.

Sprinkle with the remaining ¼ cup (50 g) sugar and bake for 10 to 12 minutes, until golden brown. Cool completely, then store airtight for up to a week.

almond sweetmeats

SOSPIRI DI MONACA

◆◆◆

Makes 30

◆◆◆

If you were the lady of an aristocratic household in Sicily during the eighteenth and nineteenth centuries, you would have access to *monache di casa*, or nuns "living at home." These were nuns who had left convents that had been closed or confiscated, or lay people who had not taken vows but had dedicated themselves to a religious life of prayer and contemplation (and baking). These women would have learned the art of pastry and confectionery in the convents, secrets that would come with them as they ventured into the outside world—or into the homes of aristocratic families.

Dolcini da riposto, meaning little sweets that are put away, is a category of sweets that are kept for when guests visit. Noble ladies would receive guests in their parlors: high-ceilinged, lavishly decorated reception rooms a floor above street level. Even today, the second floor (if you count the ground floor as the first) is called the *piano nobile*, or noble floor. Pretty little sweetmeats like these would make their appearance; jewels of different colors and flavors, decorated with colored icings, gold dragees, and crystallized flower petals, purchased at the Florio apothecaries in Palermo. Today you can find very special *dolcini* in the towns of Erice, where they are called *dolcini di Erice*; Modica, where they are called simply *dolci di riposto*; and in Palermo, where, at I Segreti del Chiostro, a former convent, they are called *sospiri di monaca*.

Unlike most of the recipes in this chapter, these dolcini aren't baked. The orange and chocolate ones are traditional, while the strawberry-rose and mulberry-jasmine are my own flights of fancy, once again using Sicilian ingredients in a new way.

 CONTINUED NEXT PAGE

the orange ones

QUELLI ALL'ARANCIA

◆◆◆

1 cup (200 g) sugar, plus ⅓ cup (60 g) for decorating

Half of a small orange, skin and all, but no seeds

2 cups (200 g) almond flour

1 teaspoon orange-blossom water

Pinch of fine sea salt

Line a baking sheet with parchment paper. Place the ⅓ cup (60 g) sugar for decorating in a shallow bowl and set aside.

In a small food processor or blender, puree the orange until smooth. You should have ¼ cup (60 ml) of puree.

In a large bowl, combine the almond flour, 1 cup (200 g) of sugar, orange-blossom water, and salt. Add the orange puree a tablespoon at a time, mixing well with a wooden spoon, until a sticky but firm dough is formed. Keep stirring to make sure everything is evenly mixed.

Pinch off little nut-sized pieces of dough and roll them into balls in the palms of your hands. Roll each ball in the sugar in the shallow bowl and place on the baking sheet. Continue with the rest of the dough. Loosely cover with a cotton towel and set aside for at least 4 and up to 12 hours. After that, store airtight for up to 2 weeks.

the chocolate ones

QUELLI DI CIOCCOLATO

◆◆◆

1¼ cups (250 g) sugar, plus ⅓ cup (60 g) for decorating

2½ cups (250 g) almond flour

3 tablespoons unsweetened cocoa

Pinch of fine sea salt

⅓ cup (80 ml) freshly brewed coffee

Line a baking sheet with parchment paper. Place the ⅓ cup (60 g) sugar for decorating in a shallow bowl and set aside.

In a large bowl, combine the almond flour, 1¼ cups (250 g) of sugar, cocoa, and salt. Add the coffee a tablespoon at a time, mixing well with a wooden spoon, until a sticky but firm dough is formed. Keep stirring to make sure everything is evenly mixed.

Pinch off little nut-sized pieces of dough and roll them into balls in the palms of your hands. Roll each ball in the sugar in the shallow bowl and place on the baking sheet. Continue with the rest of the dough. Loosely cover with a cotton towel and set aside for at least 4 and up to 12 hours. After that, store airtight for up to 2 weeks.

the mulberry-jasmine ones

QUELLI AI GELSI E GELSOMINO

◆◆◆

1¼ cups (250 g) sugar, plus ⅓ cup (60 g) for decorating

10 ripe mulberries or blackberries (about ½ cup / 70 g)

2½ cups (250 g) almond flour

½ teaspoon pure jasmine extract (see page 23)

Pinch of fine sea salt

Line a baking sheet with parchment paper. Place the ⅓ cup (60 g) sugar for decorating in a shallow bowl and set aside.

In a small food processor or blender, puree the berries. You should have ¼ cup (60 ml) of puree.

In a large bowl, combine the almond flour, 1¼ cups (250g) of sugar, jasmine extract, and salt. Add the berry puree a tablespoon at a time, mixing well with a wooden spoon, until a sticky but firm dough is formed. Keep stirring to make sure everything is evenly mixed.

Pinch off little nut-sized pieces of dough and roll them into balls in the palms of your hands. Roll each ball in the sugar in the shallow bowl and place on the baking sheet. Continue with the rest of the dough. Loosely cover with a cotton towel and set aside for at least 4 and up to 12 hours. After that, store airtight for up to 2 weeks.

the strawberry-rose ones

QUELLI ALLE FRAGOLE E ROSA

◆◆◆

1¼ cups (250 g) sugar, plus ⅓ cup (60 g) for decorating

6 strawberries (about ½ cup / 60 g)

2 tablespoons freeze-dried strawberry powder (optional, but worth it)

2½ cups (250 g) almond flour

1 tablespoon rose water

Pinch of fine sea salt

Line a baking sheet with parchment paper. Place the ⅓ cup (60 g) of sugar for decorating in a shallow bowl and set aside.

In a small food processor or blender, puree the berries with the strawberry powder. You should have ¼ cup (60 ml) of puree.

In a large bowl, combine the almond flour, 1¼ cups (250 g) of sugar, rose water, and salt. Add the berry puree a tablespoon at a time, mixing well with a wooden spoon, until a sticky but firm dough is formed. Keep stirring to make sure everything is evenly mixed.

Pinch off little nut-sized pieces of dough and roll them into balls in the palms of your hands. Roll each ball in the sugar in the shallow bowl and place on the baking sheet. Loosely cover with a cotton towel and set aside for at least 4 and up to 12 hours. After that, store airtight for up to 2 weeks.

etna mess

PASTICCIONA DELL'ETNA

◆◆◆

Serves
4

◆◆◆

It's unlikely, but you may one day find yourself with some past-their-prime fior di mandorla (page 66). You could toast them and crumble them over fruit or granita, or you could try this.

1 cup (120 g) soft berries, such as mulberries, raspberries, or blackberries

¼ cup (50 g) granulated sugar

Grated zest and juice of half a lemon

8 fior di mandorla (page 66)

1 cup (240 ml) heavy cream

¼ cup (70 g) *pasta di pistacchio* (page 212)

¼ cup (30 g) powdered sugar

In a small bowl, combine the berries, granulated sugar, and lemon zest and juice. Stir and smash until the sugar is incorporated. At this point, you can chill the mixture for up to 12 hours.

Preheat the oven to 375°F (190°C).

Place the (already baked) fior di mandorla on a small baking sheet and toast them in the oven for 5 to 8 minutes, until browned and crispy. Set aside to cool.

In another bowl, whisk together the cream, pasta di pistacchio, and powdered sugar, then whip until the mixture is billowy and just beginning to hold its shape.

In 4 individual bowls or glasses, layer half the berries with their juice, then one of the fior di mandorla, crushed slightly with your hands, then half of the pistachio cream; then repeat with the remaining berries, cookies, and cream. Drizzle with any remaining berry liquid.

little almond and cherry cookies

PASTICCINI ALLA MANDORLA E AMARENE

Makes 18

Every pastry shop with the slightest trace of an Italian accent sells these chewy little cookies with a neon-red cherry on top. While the usual glacé cherries—in a color not found in nature—have a certain appeal, I've leveled up a bit here, using Luxardo or Amarena cherries in their place.

The base recipe is followed by two variations that add some very Sicilian flavors, just arranged differently. I like to think of it as a gustatory mixtape.

2½ cups (250 g) almond flour
¾ cup (150 g) sugar
2 tablespoons honey
2 egg whites
¼ teaspoon fine sea salt
¼ teaspoon almond extract
18 pitted Luxardo or Amarena cherries in syrup, drained and patted dry

Preheat the oven to 375°F (190°C). Line a baking sheet with parchment paper.

In a large bowl, combine the almond flour, sugar, honey, egg whites, salt, and almond extract and mix well with a wooden spoon until a sticky dough forms.

Fit a cloth pastry bag with a ¾-inch (2 cm) star tip, or use a cookie press with the star disk. Fill with some of the dough and squeeze it out onto the baking sheet, forming rings 1½ inches (4 cm) in diameter. Leave a thumb-width between each one. Press a cherry into the center of each ring and bake for 10 to 12 minutes, until golden brown. Cool completely, then store airtight for up to a week.

Pasticcini Di Mandorle e Pistacchi CONTINUED NEXT PAGE

the rose ones

QUELLI ALLE ROSE

3 tablespoons powdered sugar

3 tablespoons powdered rose petals (optional, but nice)

2½ cups (250 g) almond flour

¾ cup (150 g) granulated sugar

1 tablespoon honey

1 tablespoon rose water

2 egg whites

¼ teaspoon fine sea salt

Preheat the oven to 375°F (190°C). Line a baking sheet with parchment paper.

Sift together the powdered sugar and powdered rose petals and set aside.

In a large bowl, combine the almond flour, granulated sugar, honey, rose water, egg whites and salt and mix well with a wooden spoon until a sticky dough forms.

Fit a cloth pastry bag with a ¾-inch (2 cm) star tip, or use a cookie press with the star disk. Fill with some of the dough and squeeze it out onto the baking sheet, forming rings 1½ inches (4 cm) in diameter. Leave a thumb-width between each one. Bake for 10 to 12 minutes, until golden brown. Cool for 10 minutes, then dust generously with the rose sugar. Cool completely, then store airtight for up to a week.

the saffron, lemon, and ginger ones

QUELLI ALLO ZAFFERANO, LIMONE, E ZENZERO

1 tablespoon lemon juice

⅛ teaspoon saffron threads

2½ cups (250 g) almond flour

¾ cup (150 g) sugar

Grated zest of 1 lemon

One 2-inch (5 cm) piece of ginger, peeled and grated

2 egg whites

¼ teaspoon fine sea salt

A few slices of crystallized ginger, diced, for garnish

Line a baking sheet with parchment paper. Place the lemon juice and saffron in a small cup and soak for 30 minutes.

Preheat the oven to 375°F (190°C).

In a large bowl, combine the almond flour, sugar, lemon zest, grated ginger, egg whites, and salt with the lemon juice–saffron mixture, and mix well with a wooden spoon until a sticky dough forms.

Fit a cloth pastry bag with a ¾-inch (2 cm) star tip, or use a cookie press with the star disk. Fill with some of the dough and squeeze it out onto the baking sheet, forming rings 1½ inches (4 cm) in diameter. Leave a thumb-width between each one. Press a piece of crystallized ginger into the center of each ring and bake for 10 to 12 minutes, until golden brown. Cool completely, then store airtight for up to a week.

almond eyes of saint lucy

GLI OCCHI DI SANTA LUCIA

◆◆◆

Makes 8 pair

◆◆◆

Ah, Saint Lucy, the patron saint of eyesight and light. She enjoys a huge following in Scandinavia, with celebrations in midwinter each year. Saint Lucy was a Christian girl born in Siracusa, Sicily, in the fourth century. As punishment for not renouncing her faith during the Diocletianic Persecutions, her eyes were gouged out, but her eyesight was miraculously restored. In Sicily, she gets two celebrations, in December and in May, for two separate miracles. (The other involved famine and a miraculous shipment of grain.) These chewy orange-scented almond cookies from Siracusa are made in honor of the first miracle. Best served in pairs.

Orange Pupils

2 large navel oranges

1 cup (240 ml) water

¾ cup (150 g) sugar

2 tablespoons honey

Almond Eyes

2 egg whites

¼ teaspoon fine sea salt

1 cup (200 g) sugar

½ teaspoon almond extract

2 cups (200 g) almond flour

¼ cup (30 g) powdered sugar, to finish

First, make the orange pupils. Cut the oranges into quarters. Pull the peel away from the flesh and put the peel into a small saucepan. Cover with water and bring to a boil. Turn the heat down and simmer for 30 minutes, or until the peel is very soft when pierced with a sharp knife. Drain the peel and set aside.

In the same saucepan, stir together the water, sugar and honey and bring to a boil. Add the softened peel, turn down the heat, and boil gently until the syrup is very thick and the peel is translucent, about 45 minutes. Remove the peel from the syrup and cool.

Stamp circles out of the peel with a 1-inch (2.5 cm) round cookie cutter or with the end of an apple corer. Use the syrup for cocktails or add it to seltzer.

Preheat the oven to 375°F (190°C).

In a large bowl, beat the egg whites and salt with an electric mixer until foamy and beginning to turn white. Add the sugar a spoonful at a time, continuing to beat, until all the sugar has been used. Continue to beat until stiff peaks form. Add the almond extract, then fold in the almond flour, gently but with authority, a third at a time. Divide the dough into fourths, and divide each fourth into 4 for a total of 16 pieces. With your hands, form each piece into a ½-inch (1.3 cm) thick flattened oval; pinch the ends to form almond-shaped ovals and set aside on a work surface. When they have all been formed, sift the powdered sugar over the tops. Place the ovals on the baking sheets two finger-widths apart, and press one of the orange disks into the center of each one to form the eyeball's pupil. Bake for 12 to 15 minutes, until nicely browned. Cool completely, then store airtight for up to a week.

FILLED *Pastries*

DOLCETTI RIPIENI

little cassatas

CASSATINE

◆◆◆

Makes 12

◆◆◆

In the next chapter, you'll meet the one pastry that, more than any other, bears the imprint of nearly three millennia of invasions, conquests, and dominations on Sicilian shores: the *cassata*. For now, let me present its young associate, the *cassatina*. It contains marzipan from the Arab period, ricotta brought by the Greeks, and chocolate and sponge cake from the Spanish domination. In Catania, where Saint Agatha is the patron saint, a version of these are called *minne di Sant'Agata,* or Saint Agatha's . . . breasts.

Standard muffin tins are the perfect size and shape for these little *monoporzione,* or single serving, cakes. Cherries are the most common garnish for these, but you could also use candied orange peel or bits of dried angelica or kiwi.

1 recipe *marzapane* (page 62)

Green food coloring

1 recipe *pan di Spagna* (page 133), baked in an 18- by 13-inch (46 by 33 cm) baking sheet

Soaking Syrup

½ cup (120 ml) water

½ cup (100 g) sugar

2 tablespoons Marsala, orange liqueur, or orange juice

Powdered sugar, for rolling

1 ½ recipes *crema di ricotta* (page 164)

Icing

1 egg white

1½ to 2 cups (190 to 230 g) powdered sugar

1 teaspoon lemon or orange juice

12 Luxardo, Amarena, or candied cherries

Line each of the cups of a 12-cup muffin tin individually with plastic wrap (cling film); set aside.

In a mixing bowl, knead enough green food coloring into the marzapane to turn it a nice kelly green; keep wrapped until ready to use.

To make the soaking syrup, stir together the sugar and water in a small saucepan. Bring to a boil over medium-high heat, stirring to dissolve the sugar. Boil for 1 minute, then remove from the heat and cool to room temperature before stirring in the Marsala. The syrup can be made a few days ahead and kept refrigerated.

Dust a work surface with powdered sugar. Divide the marzapane into 12 equal pieces. Roll each piece out to a strip 1½ inches (4 cm) wide and 7 inches (18 cm) long. Line the side of each cup of the muffin tin with a strip of marzapane.

With a 2-inch (5 cm) round cookie cutter, cut out 12 disks of pan di Spagna and fit one into the bottom of each cup. Brush with some of the syrup, then fill each cup with ricotta cream to about half a finger width from the top.

Cut out 12 more disks of pan di Spagna, each a little less than 3 inches (7.5 cm) in diameter, and place on top of the ricotta in each muffin cup. Cover the muffin tin with more plastic wrap and refrigerate several hours or overnight.

Before serving, make the icing. Whisk the egg white until foamy, about 1 minute. Whisk in the lemon juice and enough of the powdered sugar to make a thick icing. Keep covered while you unmold the *cassatine*.

Turn the cassatine out of the muffin tin, using the plastic wrap to coax them out; discard the wrap. Put a spoonful of icing on top of each cassatina and top with a cherry.

ATERIA - COSTANZ
DOLCERIA - GELATE
GELATERIA - COS
CERIA - GELATERI
VIA S. SPAVENTA, 7/9 - NOTO (SR) - TEL.0931-835243

spiced fig and chocolate christmas cookies

CUCCIDATI

◆◆◆

Makes 24 large or 48 small cookies

◆◆◆

There's an excellent Sicilian pasticceria in my neighborhood in Brooklyn called Monteleone, owned by a man who was born and raised in Sicily. His pastries taste as authentic as any you'll find in Sicily and, lucky for all of us, he makes *cuccidati* year-round, not just at Christmastime. (That's when he makes a larger, ring-shaped version called *buccellati,* or bracelets.) With the exception of his, I can't help thinking that the cuccidati in every other Italian American bakery are the cookie version of the game "telephone," where one person whispers a word to the next and on down the line, until the word at the end bears only a passing resemblance to the original. Most are overly sweet and figgy, without the notes of chocolate and spice, citrus and nuts that make cuccidati unique. Here they are in all their delicious complexity.

Dough

1 cup (240 g) unsalted butter, at room temperature

⅔ cup (130 g) sugar

½ teaspoon fine sea salt

2 eggs

3½ cups (420 g) all-purpose flour, or 3 cups (360 g) 00 flour

¼ cup (60 ml) milk, as needed

Filling

2 cups (300 g) soft dried figs

1 cup (240 ml) hot water

⅔ cup (130 g) sugar

¼ cup (60 ml) Marsala

2 tablespoons honey

Half an orange, skin and all, but no seeds

1 cup (120 g) toasted walnuts or almonds

⅓ cup (50 g) grated milk chocolate

1 teaspoon cinnamon

½ teaspoon ground cloves

In a large bowl, stir the butter and sugar with a wooden spoon to combine well; or use a stand mixer with the paddle attachment. Add the salt and then the eggs, one at a time, mixing well as you go. Add the flour and mix just until the dough comes together. If the dough needs a little more moisture to come together, add up to ¼ cup (60 ml) of milk a little at a time. Transfer the dough to a lightly floured surface and knead it gently a few times. Divide it into fourths, wrap the pieces in plastic wrap, and chill. The dough can be made up to 3 days ahead of time and kept in the fridge; remove it about 20 minutes before you plan to finish the cuccidati.

To make the filling, trim the tops off the figs and cut them into fourths. Transfer them to a large saucepan and add the hot water, sugar, Marsala, and honey. Coarsely chop the orange and add it to the saucepan. Simmer this mixture over medium heat for about 30 minutes, until the figs are falling-apart soft and nearly all the liquid is absorbed; there should be just a few tablespoons left in the saucepan. Set aside to cool for 15 minutes.

Meanwhile, pulse the nuts in a food processor until finely ground; transfer to a large bowl. Now pulse the soaked figs with their liquid in the food processor to form a rough paste. Scrape this into the bowl with the nuts, stir in the grated chocolate, cinnamon and cloves, and cool to room temperature. The filling can be made up to a week ahead of time and stored in an airtight container in the fridge. It's even easier to form the cuccidati when the filling is cold.

CONTINUED NEXT PAGE

Glaze

1 cup (115 g) powdered sugar

½ teaspoon fiori di Sicilia (see page 23) or vanilla extract

2 to 3 tablespoons boiling water

1 egg, for egg wash

Multicolored nonpareils

Make the glaze: in a small bowl, combine the powdered sugar, fiori di Sicilia, and 2 tablespoons of boiling water. Whisk until smooth, dribbling in more boiling water as needed. Keep this covered at room temperature until ready to use.

When you're ready to finish the operation, preheat the oven to 350°F (180°C) and line three baking sheets with parchment paper.

In a small glass, whisk the egg with 2 tablespoons of water to make an egg wash. Have ready a pastry brush and a very sharp knife or straight razor blade.

On a lightly floured board, roll out a fourth of the dough into an 18- by 3-inch (46 by 7.5 cm) rectangle. Brush the edges with egg wash. Spoon one-fourth of the filling down the middle of the dough lengthwise. Fold the dough over to enclose the filling and bring the edges together, then carefully roll the log over so the seam side is underneath. Repeat with the other three pieces of dough and the rest of the filling.

Now you have a choice to get fancy or keep it simple.

For the simplest option, cut each log crosswise into 12 pieces. Transfer the pieces to the baking sheets, leaving two finger-widths between each one. Bake for 20 to 25 minutes or until nicely browned. Cool, then drizzle with glaze and sprinkle with nonpareils.

To get fancy, flatten each log slightly with your hand and cut it crosswise into 6 pieces, each about 3 inches (7.5 cm) wide. With the knife or razor, make cuts crosswise all the way through to the work surface, leaving one side of the log uncut, as though you're making fringe. Now separate each little piece of the "fringe" from its neighbors and curl it this way and that. There's no specific design, just let your fancy be your guide. As you finish each piece, carefully transfer it to one of the baking sheets, leaving two finger-widths between each one of the cuccidati. Bake for 25 to 30 minutes, or until nicely browned. Let cool, then drizzle with glaze and sprinkle with nonpareils. Store airtight for up to a week.

cream-filled pastries

GENOVESI

Makes 8

From the sixteenth century to the eighteenth, the Genoese carried on a brisk trade with Sicily, primarily in the abundant wheat that, in ancient Rome, had lent Sicily the nickname "Granary of Rome." It is said that during this time, a young nun took a fancy to a Genoese sailor in Trapani and created these pastries in tribute to him, his hat, and their unrequited love.

Genovesi are a specialty of the western part of the island, and excellent ones are to be found at the Pasticceria Maria Grammatico in Erice. Anyone with even the slightest knowledge of Sicilian sweets knows about Ms. Grammatico, the octogenarian who, as a young girl, learned the art of pastry-making from the sisters at the Convento di San Carlo. In 1964, with only three kilos of almonds and the help of her mother and siblings, she opened her tiny *laboratorio* (not so tiny anymore!), where for almost sixty years she has created exquisite Sicilian pastries, just as she learned from the nuns. Maria says genovesi should be eaten still warm from the oven, and I agree.

1 recipe *pasta frolla* (page 135)

1 recipe pistachio and jasmine filling *or* vanilla and orange-blossom filling (recipes follow)

1 egg, for egg wash

Powdered sugar, for dusting

If your pasta frolla is freshly made, chill it for an hour before you use it. If you've made it ahead of time, take it out of the fridge 20 minutes before you plan to use it. If your filling is freshly made, proceed with the pastry preparation. If it's been in the fridge, take it out 20 minutes before you plan to use it.

When you are ready to bake the pastries, preheat the oven to 375°F (190°C). Line two baking sheets with parchment paper. Whisk the egg and 1 tablespoon of water together in a small glass to make an egg wash; have ready a pastry brush.

On a lightly floured surface, roll out a fourth of the dough into a 12- by 4-inch (30 by 10 cm) rectangle. With a 3-inch (7.5 cm) round cookie cutter, cut out four circles of dough. Place two of the circles on a baking sheet, leaving two finger-widths between them. Brush with the egg wash and place a nice big spoonful of filling in the center of each dough circle. Carefully press the remaining circles of dough on top to enclose the filling. Trim each pastry with the cookie cutter to neaten up the edges. Repeat with the other three portions of dough. Gather and reroll the scraps to make one more genovese.

Bake for 15 to 20 minutes, or until nicely browned. Dust with the powdered sugar just before serving. These are best served warm or at room temperature. Store airtight in the fridge for up to 3 days.

CONTINUED NEXT PAGE

the pistachio and jasmine ones

QUELLI AL PISTACCHIO E GELSOMINO

◆◆◆

⅓ cup (70 g) sugar

1 tablespoon cornstarch

Pinch of salt

3 egg yolks

1 cup (240 ml) milk

¼ teaspoon almond extract

4 drops jasmine extract (see page 23), or 1 teaspoon rose water

1 tablespoon pistachio butter, (see page 212)

In a small bowl, whisk together the sugar, cornstarch, and salt. In a larger bowl, whisk the eggs for about a minute, until they start to become lighter in color. Whisk in the sugar mixture a little at a time until smooth. The mixture will be thick.

In a medium saucepan over medium heat, bring the milk just to a boil. As soon as the milk reaches a boil, pour it slowly into the egg mixture, whisking constantly. When all the milk is added, pour the mixture back into the saucepan. Over medium heat, bring the mixture slowly back up to a boil, whisking constantly. When it begins to thicken, turn the heat down a bit and let it simmer, still whisking, until it's completely thickened, another couple of minutes. Take it off the heat and add the almond and jasmine extracts and the pistachio butter, whisking to combine well and release steam.

Immediately place plastic wrap directly on the surface of the filling to prevent a skin from forming. Use the filling right away, or store it in the fridge for up to a week.

the vanilla and orange-blossom ones

QUELLI ALLA VANIGLIA E ZAGARA

◆◆◆

¼ cup (50 g) sugar

1 tablespoon cornstarch

Pinch of salt

3 egg yolks

1 cup (240 ml) milk

½ teaspoon vanilla extract

1 teaspoon orange-blossom water

1 tablespoon finely chopped candied orange peel (see page 210)

In a small bowl, whisk together the sugar, cornstarch, and salt. In a larger bowl, whisk the eggs for about a minute, until they start to become lighter in color. Whisk in the sugar mixture a little at a time until smooth. The mixture will be thick.

In a medium saucepan over medium heat, bring the milk just to a boil. As soon as the milk reaches a boil, pour it slowly into the egg mixture, whisking constantly. When all the milk is added, pour the mixture back into the saucepan. Over medium heat, bring the mixture slowly back up to a boil, whisking constantly. When it begins to thicken, turn the heat down a bit and let it simmer, still whisking, until it's completely thickened, another couple of minutes. Take it off the heat and add the vanilla extract and orange-blossom water, whisking to combine well and release steam. Stir in the candied orange zest.

Immediately place plastic wrap directly on the surface of the filling to prevent a skin from forming. Use the filling right away, or store it in the fridge for up to a week.

mandarin orange–almond cookies

NACATULI EOLIANI

◆◆◆

Makes 24

◆◆◆

These cookies are still the domain of women in the Aeolian Islands, Lipari in particular. During late autumn, women get together in pairs or groups to craft these beauties, decorating them using small metal pincers called *pizzicaloru*. One November in Lipari, at the Pasticceria Subba, I was fortunate enough to come upon two sisters huddled over a table, chattering away and making *nacatuli*. They were works of art, those nacatuli, adorned with pastry curlicues and tiny roses and intricate designs created with the pincers.

Back in the U.S., I tried in vain to find the pincers until I broadened my search to include Middle Eastern and Turkish shops. That opened the door to pincers, pincers, everywhere pincers. They're used to decorate cookies called *ma'amoul*—filled with dates, walnuts, and floral waters—that bear a striking resemblance to nacatuli. Search online for "pastry pincher," "ma'amoul pincher," or "pastry crimper"; they're 2 to 3 inches (5 to 7.5 cm) long and look like tongs with serrated edges.

Thankfully, the art of nacatuli is being preserved by groups of Aeolian women who hold nacatuli competitions in early December in Lipari, spurred on by "likes" on TikTok and YouTube.

Dough

1 cup (240 g) unsalted butter, at room temperature

⅔ cup (130 g) sugar

½ teaspoon fine sea salt

2 eggs

3½ cups (420 g) all-purpose flour, or 3 cups (360 g) 00 flour

¼ cup (60 ml) milk, or Malvasia, Marsala, or other sweet wine, as needed

In a large bowl, mix the butter and sugar, stirring with a wooden spoon to combine well; or use a stand mixer with the paddle attachment. Add the salt, then add the eggs one at a time, mixing well as you go. Add the flour all at once and mix just until the dough comes together. If the dough needs a little more moisture to come together, add up to ¼ cup (60 ml) of milk a little at a time. Transfer the dough to a lightly floured surface and knead it gently a few times. Divide the dough into fourths, wrap each in plastic wrap, and chill until you're ready to bake the nacatuli. The dough can be made up to 3 days ahead of time and kept in the fridge. Remove it about 20 minutes before you plan to use it.

CONTINUED NEXT PAGE

FARINA DI GRANO TENERO
TIPO "00"
GRAN
MUGNAIO
CONSIGLIATA
PER DOLCI
MOLINO
Spadoni
prova le nostre ricette!

Filling

1½ cups (250 g) blanched almonds

¾ cup (150 g) sugar

¼ cup (60 ml) orange or mandarin juice (from 1 orange or mandarin)

2 tablespoons orange liqueur or Malvasia

1 tablespoon honey

Grated zest of 1 mandarin, or half a lemon and half a small orange

½ teaspoon cinnamon

¼ teaspoon fine sea salt

1 egg white

1 egg, for egg wash

To make the filling, first preheat the oven to 350°F (180°C).

Coarsely chop the almonds and spread them in an even layer on a baking sheet. Toast for 6 to 8 minutes, or until browned and fragrant. Let them cool completely and chop them as finely as you can, but don't pulverize. Transfer the almonds to a large bowl and add the sugar, citrus juice, liqueur, honey, zest, cinnamon, salt, and egg white, stirring to combine well. The filling can be made up to 1 week ahead; store it airtight in the fridge. It's even easier to work with the filling when it's cold.

When you're ready to bake, preheat the oven to 350°F (180°C). Line three baking sheets with parchment paper, and have ready a pastry brush, a sharp knife, and your pincers.

Whisk the egg with 2 tablespoons of water in a small glass to make an egg wash.

On a lightly floured surface, roll out a fourth of the dough into a 12- by 5-inch (30 by 13 cm) rectangle. With a 2-inch (5 cm) round or oval cookie cutter, cut out 12 pieces. Set the scraps aside for decorating the nacatuli. Place 6 of the pieces on a baking sheet, leaving two finger-widths between each. Brush with egg wash and place a tablespoon of filling in the center of each. Carefully press the other 6 pieces of dough on top. If you like, cut decorative slits into the tops of the nacatuli and use pincers or pie crimpers to embellish the dough. If you're feeling especially creative and industrious, pinch off tiny pieces of the reserved dough scraps and form them into roses to decorate the nacatuli. More is more here, but don't feel you have to go overboard; they're just as delicious, simply adorned.

Bake for 25 to 30 minutes, until lightly browned. Let cool before storing airtight at room temperature for up to a week, or frozen up to a month.

pistachio-filled holiday cookies

NACATULI BRONTESI

Makes 24

Bronte is the pistachio center of Sicily, so it makes sense that pistachios are the town's nut of choice. These aren't fancifully decorated like nacatuli eoliani (though you could fancy them up) or iced and sprinkled with nonpareils, like cuccidati (though you could do that too). They don't need tarting up, especially if you can get your hands on Bronte pistachios. Homemade rose-petal liqueur (page 229) would make such a nice accompaniment at a holiday dinner, don't you think?

Dough

1 cup (240 g) unsalted butter, at room temperature

⅔ cup (130 g) granulated sugar

½ teaspoon fine sea salt

2 eggs

3½ cups (420 g) all-purpose flour, or 3 cups (360 g) 00 flour

¼ cup (60 ml) milk, as needed

Filling

2 cups (250 g) lightly toasted pistachios

¾ cup (150 g) sugar

1 tablespoon rose water or jasmine extract (see page 23)

½ teaspoon ground cloves

¼ teaspoon fine sea salt

1 egg white

1 egg, for egg wash

Powdered sugar, for dusting

In a large bowl, mix the butter and granulated sugar, stirring with a wooden spoon to combine well; or use a stand mixer with the paddle attachment.

Add the salt and then the eggs one at a time, mixing well as you go. Add the flour and mix just until the dough comes together. If the dough needs a little more moisture to come together, add up to ¼ cup (60 ml) of milk a little at a time. Transfer the dough to a lightly floured surface and knead it gently a few times. Divide the dough into fourths, wrap each in plastic wrap, and chill until you're ready to bake the nacatuli. The dough can be made up to 3 days ahead of time and kept in the fridge. Remove it about 20 minutes before you plan to use it.

To make the filling, chop the pistachios as finely as you can, but don't pulverize. Transfer them to a medium bowl and add the sugar, rose water, cloves, salt, and egg white, stirring to combine well. The filling can be made up to 1 week ahead; store it airtight in the fridge. It's even easier to work with the filling when it's cold.

When you're ready to bake, preheat the oven to 350°F (180°C), line three baking sheets with parchment paper, and have a pastry brush ready. Whisk the egg with 2 tablespoons of water in a small glass to make an egg wash.

On a lightly floured surface, roll out a fourth of the dough into a 12- by 5-inch (30 by 13 cm) rectangle. With a 2-inch (5 cm) round or oval cookie cutter, cut out 12 pieces of dough. Place 6 of the pieces on a baking sheet, leaving two finger-widths between each. Brush with egg wash and place a tablespoon of filling in the center of each. Carefully press the other 6 pieces of dough on top. If you like, cut decorative slits in the tops of the nacatuli and use pincers (more on those in the headnote for mandarin orange–almond cookies, page 90) to embellish them.

Bake for 25 to 30 minutes, or until lightly browned. Cool completely, then dust with powdered sugar. Store airtight at room temperature for up to a week.

ricotta pastries for saint agatha

MINNE DI SANT'AGATA

◆◆◆

Makes 8 or 9

◆◆◆

Sicilians have a profound fascination with death, suffering, miracles, and fate, and many pastries in the Sicilian culinary pantheon were created to commemorate these preoccupations—as though they contain within them a certain homeopathic healing power. And true to character, the darker the suffering, the more dazzling the pastry.

Saint Agatha, patron saint of Catania, was a fifteen-year-old girl from a noble Sicilian family. She had dedicated her life to God and taken a vow of chastity. Agatha, alas, caught the eye of a Roman prelate sent to rule Sicily. She spurned his advances, maintaining her vow of purity even when jailed and viciously tortured. Finally, the prelate ordered her breasts cut off, but even that didn't work. Agatha died a virgin martyr in the year 251. She's often depicted in paintings carrying her breasts on a plate. In 2020, Italian street artist TVBoy painted a likeness of Saint Agatha on one of the walls of the open-air fish market in Catania. It's still there today, near an arched passageway by the swordfish.

1 recipe pasta frolla (page 135)

Icing

2 cups (230 g) powdered sugar

3 tablespoons, unsalted butter, melted

2 tablespoons milk

¼ teaspoon fiori di Sicilia (see page 23), or ½ teaspoon vanilla extract

1 egg, for egg wash

½ recipe crema di ricotta (page 164), made without the whipped cream

8 to 10 maraschino, Luxardo, or Amarena cherries

If your pasta frolla is freshly made, chill it for an hour before you use it. If you've made it ahead of time, take it out of the fridge 20 minutes before you plan to use it.

To make the icing, in a medium bowl, whisk together the powdered sugar, melted butter, milk, and fiori di Sicilia until smooth. Keep covered until ready to use.

Preheat the oven to 375°F (190°C). Line two baking sheets with parchment paper. Whisk the egg and 1 tablespoon of water together in a small glass to make an egg wash, and have ready a pastry brush.

On a lightly floured surface, roll out a fourth of the dough into a 12- by 4-inch (30 by 10 cm) rectangle. With a 3-inch (7.5 cm) round cookie cutter, cut out four circles. Place two of the circles on a baking sheet, leaving two finger-widths between them. Brush them with egg wash and place a nice big spoonful of crema di ricotta in the center of each. Carefully press the other two pieces of dough on top to enclose the filling. Trim each pastry with the cookie cutter to neaten up the edges. Repeat with the other three portions of dough. Gather and re-roll the scraps to make one more minne.

Bake for 15 to 20 minutes, or until nicely browned. Cool completely, then pour icing on each minne with a large spoon, spreading it with a palette or butter knife to cover as much of the pastry as you can. Once the icing has set, about 30 minutes, top each minne with a cherry nipple.

Store airtight in the fridge for up to 3 days; serve at room temperature.

Dove è più nero il lutto, ivi è più flagrante la luce.
Where the suffering is darkest, the light is most dazzling.

—GESUALDO BUFALINI,
EXPLAINING SICILIAN PESSIMISM

CS

TVBOY

CIOCCOLATO DI MODICA

MODICAN CHOCOLATE

I am not a chocolate person. That is to say, I have an appreciation for chocolate but not a taste for it (aside from the occasional Cadbury Fruit & Nut bar). Ironically—for an island so entrenched in sweets—Sicily's with me on this. But that makes sense when you think of how relatively recently chocolate arrived here and how tightly Sicilians cling to The Way Things Have Always Been Done.

Chocolate—or more accurately, cacao—came to Sicily, and more precisely the town of Modica, by way of Spanish galleons returning from the New World in the sixteenth century. This was the period of Spanish conquest of both Sicily *and* Mesoamerica. The Contea di Modica was a powerful feudal territory, stocked with nobility and aristocracy who could well afford to indulge their tastes for the novel, and cacao would become a symbol of status and power.

Modican chocolate is made from little more than cacao and sugar, crafted "a freddo," or cold-worked. Cacao beans and sugar are ground manually and never heated above 40°C (104°F), producing a chocolate that retains its flavor compounds, with a pleasant crunch from the sugar that remains undissolved. It is virtually identical to the tablets of crunchy chocolate found in Mexico, Guatemala, and parts of Spain today.

The story of Modican chocolate has it coming directly from the Aztecs, which is charming, but not altogether accurate. While grinding the cacao on a *metate* (a stone-grinding slab) is a technique used by the Aztecs, the full story is much more textured. Aztec *xocolatl* was a bitter drink, made from a base of ground cacao beans and water and sometimes thickened with ground corn. It was not sweetened and not eaten in its solid state. Sugar wasn't even known in Mesoamerica until those same conquistadors brought it with them from the Canary Islands by way of Cuba, both under Spanish domination at the time. It was back in Spain that sugar was added to the cacao, and the resulting chocolate was formed into tablets and eaten by nobility as a sweet delicacy on special occasions.

Today, Sicily's chocolate production remains concentrated in the lovely Baroque town of Modica. On my first trip there, in 1999, I visited the Antica Dolceria Bonajuto, where the Ruta family has upheld the tradition of authentic Modican chocolate since 1880. The *dolceria* was as much a museum as a shop, with burnished mahogany cabinets holding meticulous vignettes of antique and pre-Columbian chocolate paraphernalia, and two dedicated workers toiling away in the laboratory, hand-forming chocolate pastries one by one. On a visit all these years later, the crowd at Bonajuto was three deep at the counter, and those pastries were handed to me in a pretty, albeit prepacked, gift box. Modica's main street is full of chocolate shops complete with chocolate-themed magnets and chocolate-obsessed tourists.

Had Sicily not clung so zealously to chocolate in its medieval form, Sicilian chocolate might have continued evolving into the smooth tempered chocolate most of the world knows and be a bigger part of the sweets story now. But then, this ain't Switzerland, and doing things the way everyone else does isn't the Sicilian way.

Modican chocolate remains as it was five hundred years ago, when this culinary cross-pollination occurred. In 2017, a consortium of twenty local Modican chocolate producers applied for EU protection of Modican chocolate under the IGP (Indicazione Geografica Protetta) designation. The designation was granted in 2018, indicating that any chocolate claiming to be Modican must be produced, processed, or prepared only in the town of Modica.

I like it coarsely grated over gelato or the chocolate *cremolata* on page 184, where its crunchy texture can be best appreciated.

Modica

modican chocolate and meat pastries

MPANATIGGHI

◆◆◆

Makes 24

◆◆◆

Being a traveling monk in sixteenth-century Sicily couldn't have been easy. During Lent, the season of austerity preceding Easter, monks were expected to hike on foot day after day for forty days, ministering to the faithful across the land. Although they were able to stop at monasteries for sustenance, eating meat was prohibited. There is a story of Benedictine nuns in a monastery in Modica who skirted the Lenten laws by sneaking meat into a chocolate *empanadilla* (Sicily was under Spanish rule at the time) to fortify the brothers, and that's how this pastry was purportedly invented. The name *'mpanatigghi* is obviously one degree away from empanadilla.

'Mpanatigghi aren't as odd as they may sound. Think of them as a sort of mincemeat. The chocolate pretty much takes over the flavor, with spices further obscuring the taste of meat, bolstering the story of the wily Benedictine nuns. The best ones are to be found at the Antica Dolceria Bonajuto in Modica—especially when they're straight from the oven.

1 recipe pasta frolla (page 135)

Filling

8 ounces (225 g) triple-ground beef (20 percent fat)

1 cup (100 g) almond flour

5 ounces (150 g) Modican chocolate (see page 100), Mexican chocolate, or any dark chocolate, grated

Scant ½ cup (80 g) sugar

2 teaspoons vanilla extract

1 teaspoon cinnamon

½ teaspoon ground cloves

½ teaspoon fine sea salt

1 egg, for egg wash

If your pasta frolla is freshly made, chill it for an hour before you use it. If you've made it ahead of time, take it out of the fridge 20 minutes before you plan to use it.

To make the filling, place the beef, almond flour, chocolate, sugar, vanilla, cinnamon, cloves, and salt in a medium bowl and stir with a wooden spoon until the mixture comes together in a mass. Now pick up the whole mass with your hand and, with force and authority, slap it back into the bowl. Do this another 20 times. This will tenderize the meat and make the filling smooth.

Preheat the oven to 375°F (190°C). Line two baking sheets with parchment paper, and have ready a pastry brush and a sharp knife. In a glass, whisk together the egg and 2 tablespoons of water with a fork to make an egg wash.

On a lightly floured surface, roll out one-fourth of the dough ⅛ inch (3 mm) thick and punch out rounds with a 4-inch (10 cm) cookie cutter. Lift away the dough scraps and set aside.

Brush the rounds with egg wash and place a spoonful of filling in the center of each. Fold the dough over to form half-moons, enclosing the filling. Press the edges gently to adhere. With a sharp knife, cut a small slit in the top of each pastry and transfer them to the baking sheets, leaving two finger-widths between the pastries. Gather and re-roll the scraps, and continue cutting and filling pastries until all the dough and filling are used up.

Bake for 30 to 35 minutes, or until nicely browned. Cool the pastries completely before serving. Store airtight in the fridge for up to a week.

CANNOLI & Friends

CANNOLI E SUOI AMICI

cannoli

CANNOLI

◆◆◆

Makes 12

◆◆◆

I don't think it's an overstatement to say that cannoli are fetishized, and not only by Sicilians. Aside from the multisensory experience of biting into the crispy shell, releasing a wisp of powdered sugar before you hit the creamy ricotta filling, and the bits of chocolate and chewy *zuccata* or candied orange peel, there's a perfectly good reason for the obsession.

Although the exact origins of cannoli are lost somewhere between history and lore, their shape is believed to be fashioned after an ancient Greek fertility symbol whose shape is itself fashioned after ... you get it. In Piana degli Albanesi, where the best ones are said to be made, it is common to find cannoli as big as your arm or large cannoli filled with baby ones, but those are just for the spectacle of it: you can't mess with the ratio or the whole experience is lost. If you find yourself in Siracusa feeling peckish, you might consider a visit to Alfio Neri. There, chef Francesco Neri offers what he calls "cannoli therapy." This is a strictly prescribed multistep program that encourages the patient to savor each element of their cannoli (which are admittedly exquisite) one by one and slowly, as Neri tells you the qualities of each element, where they hail from, and why they are where they are. At the end of your therapy session, you are meant to feel—what? I'd have to have therapy to get over the trauma of having to listen to someone mansplain cannoli while I'm trying to eat one.

My sister's mother-in-law is Sicilian but lives in Northern Italy. I visited her once when she lived in a charming villa on the outskirts of Padova; now she's in a very chic apartment in the city center. She is so serious about her cannoli that she designed a special cannoli workstation that retracts neatly into a cabinet when not in use. This recipe is how she makes her cannoli.

One more thing: In Sicily, most people use pieces of untreated bamboo stalk, cut into 5-inch (13 cm) lengths, instead of metal cannoli tubes. The bamboo stalks float and are porous, so the cannoli shells cook evenly from both the inside and the outside. You can use them over and over, even though they'll darken with use, and they cool off faster than metal. Besides, bamboo grows 1½ inches (4 cm) per hour, so it's the ultimate in sustainability! If you do use metal cannoli tubes, the most readily available ones will be 5 inches (13 cm) long by about an inch (2.5 cm) in diameter. Buy a lot of them so you're not wasting time waiting for them to cool before you can form more cannoli.

Shells

2 cups (240 g) all-purpose flour, or 1¾ cups (210 g) 00 flour

3 tablespoons sugar

½ teaspoon cinnamon

¼ teaspoon fine sea salt

¼ cup (50 g) cold vegetable shortening or lard

2 eggs

½ cup (120 ml) whisky, Marsala, or white wine, divided

Canola, sunflower, or other neutral oil for deep-frying

1 recipe crema di ricotta (page 164), made without the whipped cream

¾ cup (180 ml) heavy cream

Chopped chocolate, mini chocolate chips, chopped pistachios, glacé or Luxardo cherries, candied orange peel, or candied watermelon rind—as you wish—to finish

Powdered sugar, to serve

To make the shells, whisk the flour, sugar, cinnamon, and salt in a large bowl to combine. With your fingertips, work the shortening or lard into the flour mixture until the dough mixture is crumbly and no bits are larger than a pea.

Separate one of the eggs and place the yolk in a medium bowl and the white in a small glass. Set the glass with the white aside and break the other egg into the bowl with the yolk. Add half of the whisky and stir to combine.

Make a well in the center of the flour mixture and pour in the egg and whisky mixture. Using a fork, gradually work in the flour mixture, mixing in a circular motion to nudge the flour into the well. Continue mixing the flour mixture into the liquid until the dough is fully incorporated and becomes hard to mix. Add the rest of the whisky and mix until the dough comes together. It will be firm. Turn the dough out onto a lightly floured surface and knead until smooth, about 3 minutes. Wrap the dough in plastic and chill for at least 1 hour or up to 12 hours.

Pour enough oil into an 8-quart (8 L) stockpot or dutch oven to come 2 inches (5 cm) up the sides. Fit a thermometer to the side of the pan and place over medium-high heat until the thermometer registers 375°F (190°C).

Meanwhile, divide the dough in half. Roll out the first half on a lightly floured surface as thinly as you can. (You should be able to see the *gazzetto* through it, but not read the words.) You can also roll the dough through a pasta machine set to the second thinnest setting. Punch out rounds of dough with a 4-inch (10 cm) cookie cutter. Gather and reroll the scraps and cut out more. Keep the dough rounds loosely covered as you work.

Now whisk the reserved egg white with a fork to loosen it. Roll out each dough round in one direction to form an oval. Prick the dough in a few places with a fork (so the cannoli don't explode when you fry them). Brush some of the egg white onto the long edge of one of the dough ovals and wrap the dough loosely around a 5-inch (13 cm) metal *cannolo* form or piece of untreated bamboo, laying the tube along the long edge of the oval. Overlap the edges of the wrapped dough a little and press so they stick together. Transfer to a parchment-lined baking sheet as you go.

Line another baking sheet with a double layer of paper towels. Fry the shells on their forms, nudging them around in the oil to color evenly, until deep golden brown, 4 to 5 minutes. Transfer to the prepared baking sheet. Let the shells cool slightly, then slip them from the forms. If you use metal tubes, let them cool until they're easy to handle before using them again. Continue this operation until all the shells are fried, then let the shells cool completely.

When you are ready to fill the cannoli, take the crema di ricotta base out of the fridge. In a separate bowl, whip the heavy cream into stiff peaks and fold it into the ricotta cream.

Fill a pastry bag with the ricotta cream and snip off the end (or use a large round tip). Working from the center to one end of a shell, pipe in the filling, then turn the shell around and pipe from the center to the opposite end. Garnish however you like with chopped chocolate, mini chocolate chips, chopped pistachios, glacé or Luxardo cherries, and/or candied orange peel, and dust with powdered sugar just before serving.

UNHOLY *Cannoli*

What if we applied the theory of deconstructivist cooking—breaking down a traditional dish into its individual elements and presenting those components in a new and different form while not altering the core nature of the dish—to cannoli? Strips of dough could be cut with a fluted pastry cutter and fried without having to form shells. Dust those with powdered sugar, then make the crema di ricotta, which you'd serve in dainty little coupes or form into cheffy pucks on plates that are disproportionately large, garnished with a chocolate curl, some chopped pistachios, a strip of candied orange peel, and a shower of those pastry strips.

I am sure that if I advocated for this, I would incur the wrath of Sicily, so I am simply posing the question: What *if*?

Asked and answered. On my latest trip to Sicily, I saw *cannoli scomposti*, or deconstructed cannoli, on two different menus. So maybe I wouldn't be so far off after all.

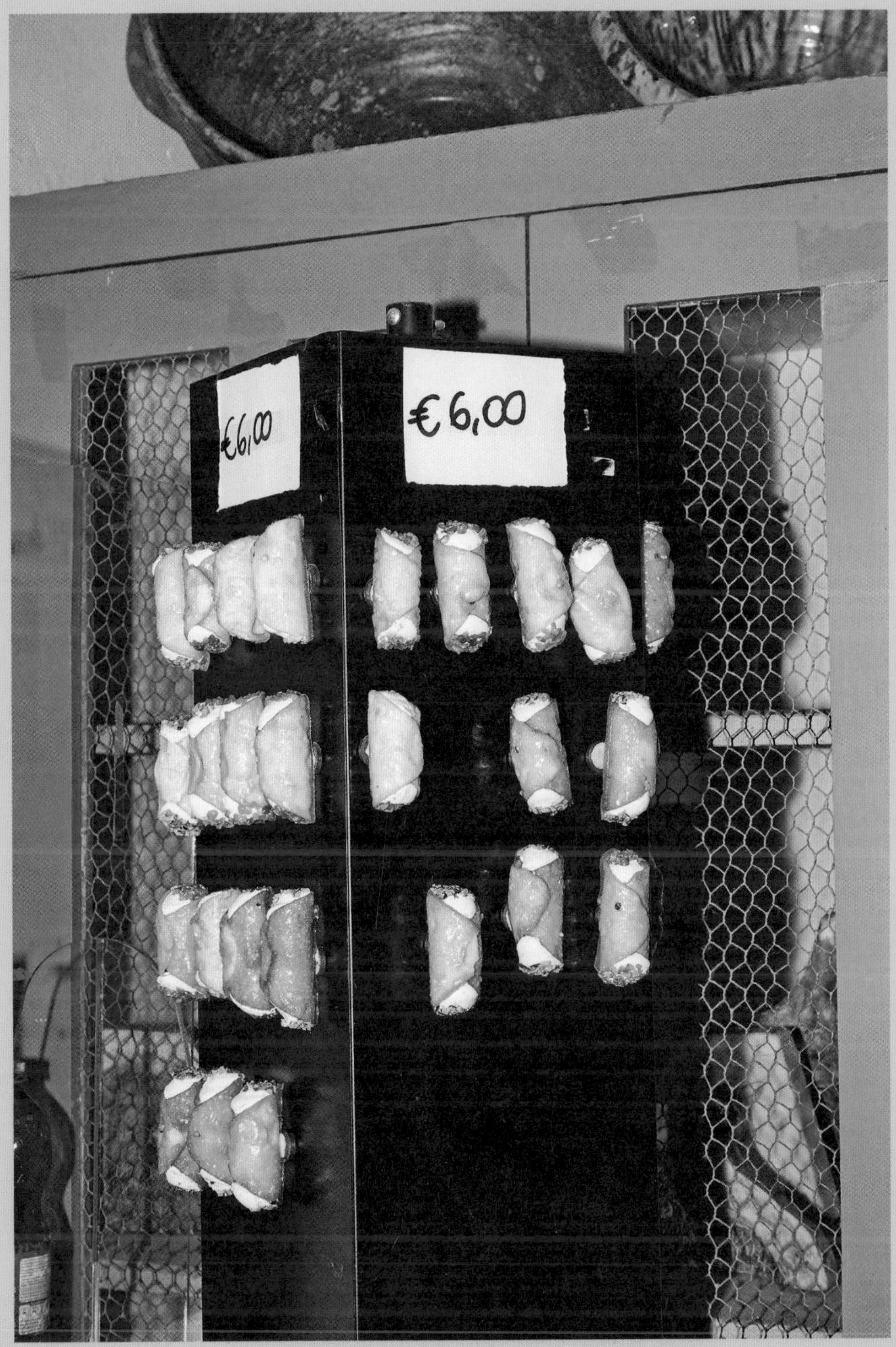
€6,00
€6,00

crispy pastry strips

CHIACCHIERE

◆◆◆

Makes about 30

◆◆◆

If someone invites you to *fare due chiacchiere,* it means they'd like to have a quick chat. *Quattro chiacchiere* is a longer commitment, usually involving a bit of gossip and a beverage. Chiacchiere is an onomatopoetic word meaning "chatter," and that's the sound these strips of dough make when they're sizzling in hot oil.

1 recipe cannoli shells (see page 107)

Canola, sunflower, or other neutral oil for deep-frying

Powdered sugar, to serve

Make a batch of dough for cannoli shells, but instead of cutting out circles, use a pastry wheel or pizza cutter to cut strips of dough about 1½ inches (4 cm) wide by 4 inches (10 cm) long. Now cut a slit down the length of each dough strip in the center, almost all the way to the ends: this keeps the chiacchiere from flipping back over when you fry them. Fry in 4 inches (10 cm) of oil heated to 375°F (190°C), turning once, until puffed and golden brown, about 3 minutes total. Remove to a paper towel–lined baking sheet as you fry them. When cool, dust with powdered sugar. These are best eaten the day they are made.

choux pastry puffs

BIGNÈ

◆◆◆

Makes
14

◆◆◆

A little *bignè* backstory: In 1768, Maria Carolina, sister of Marie Antoinette, became the queen consort to King Ferdinand of Naples and Sicily, ruling from the Palazzo Reale in Naples. The fifteen-year-old queen was Austrian-born and had refined tastes of the more northern sort. (Also, she gave birth to eighteen children in twenty-one years, far outperforming her royal duty to produce heirs.) When, in 1799, Napoleon's army invaded Naples, the king and queen and their court sought refuge in Sicily. M. C. didn't care much for the food there, so French chefs were imported to the royal court in Palermo. These chefs became known as *monsù,* or "monsieur" with a Sicilian accent. The aristocracy, now having royalty in their midst, followed Maria Carolina's lead, tripping over themselves to outdo one another with the splendor of their tables. And with that, French choux pastry entered the Sicilian kitchen.

The name bignè is a corruption of the French word *beignet*, the fried form of choux pastry. Bignè are actually quite simple to make *if* you measure precisely and do exactly what I say. No improvising here. They can be baked and filled with a creamy filling like the *testa di turco* on the next pages, or fried, like the *sfinci* found later in this book.

Bignè dough can be made up to 1 day in advance and kept airtight in the fridge. Take it out of the fridge about 20 minutes before baking.

CONTINUED NEXT PAGE

GLASOVER FONDENTE
Cod.7904
LineaProfession

1 cup (120 g) bread flour or 0 (Manitoba) flour (see page 21)

1 cup (240 ml) water or milk

½ cup (120 g) unsalted butter, at room temperature

½ teaspoon fine sea salt

4 eggs

Line two baking sheets with parchment paper. Measure out the flour before you start and have it and a wooden spoon next to the stove.

In a heavy-bottomed medium saucepan, combine the water or milk, butter, and salt and bring to a boil over medium-high heat. As soon as the mixture comes to a full rolling boil, remove the pan from the heat and add the flour all at once. With a wooden spoon, strength, and a sense of urgency, stir until the mixture comes away from the sides of the pan and forms a nice smooth mass. It won't look likely at first, but stick with it. Let the dough sit, pan loosely draped with a cotton towel, for 10 minutes.

Preheat the oven to 400°F (200°C).

This next part is easiest done in a stand mixer with the paddle attachment on medium speed, but doing it by hand is good for your self-confidence. Break the eggs into a glass measuring cup and gently beat them with a fork to combine. Pour one-fourth of the eggs into the pan with the dough and have at it with your wooden spoon (do not be tempted to use a whisk), stirring and bashing the dough against the sides of the pan until the egg is absorbed. It will look curdled at first but will come together. Continue with the rest of the eggs, stirring and bashing all the while. (Or, as I said, you could follow the same procedure but let the stand mixer do the bashing.) Scrape the sides of the pan with a silicone spatula as you go.

Once all the eggs are incorporated, dip a spoon (or a 2-ounce/60 ml ice cream scoop) in water, scoop up about ¼ cup (60 ml) of the dough, and, with the help of another spoon, push it onto the baking sheet in a mound. Continue with the rest of the dough, leaving three finger-widths between each mound and between the dough and the edges of the pan. Flick a bit of water once or twice over the balls and put the baking sheet in the oven. *Do not open the oven* while the puffs are baking. Bake for 25 minutes, then lower the oven to 350°F (180°C) for another 20 minutes. Turn off the oven—*do not open it yet*—but leave the bignè in for a final 15 minutes. Finally, remove from the oven and cool completely before filling, or wrap airtight and freeze for up to a month. The bignè will lose their crispness, but 5 minutes on a baking sheet in a 400°F (200°C) oven will crisp them right up.

chocolate-filled pastry puffs

TESTA DI TURCO

Makes 8

I'd like to think that these are named "Turk's head" out of affection, but I'm pretty sure they're not. From the ninth to the eleventh centuries, Sicily was ruled by Saracens, which is to say any person—Arab, Turkish, or otherwise—who professed the Muslim faith. The First Crusade was provoked by the Turks and ended with the Normans seizing power from the Saracens and capturing Sicily. Eating the symbolic head of your enemy seems like just desserts.

Bignè dough can be made up to one day in advance and kept airtight in the fridge. Take it out of the fridge about twenty minutes before baking.

1 recipe bignè dough (page 115)

½ cup (120 ml) heavy cream

2 recipes *crema al cioccolato* (page 166), chilled

¼ cup (30 g) powdered sugar, to finish

Preheat the oven to 400°F (200°C). On two pieces of parchment paper, use a pencil to trace four 3-inch (7.5 cm) circles onto each sheet, leaving three finger-widths between each one and the edges of the paper (and thus to the edges of the pans). Place these upside down onto two baking sheets; you should be able to see the circles through the paper.

Scrape the bignè dough into a pastry bag with a large star tip to form the puffs. (You'll have to do this in a few batches unless you have a massive pastry bag.)

Move the bag in a spiral motion to form four mounds 3 inches (7.5 cm) in diameter atop the circles you traced on the parchment, starting from the outside of each circle and moving into the middle and covering the whole surface of the circle. Squeeze out a bit of dough to fill any gaps, making sure the overall height of each circle is the same. Now pipe out a smaller circle on top of the large one. Once you have filled both baking sheets, flick some water from your fingertips over the pans and transfer to the oven. *Do not open the oven* while the puffs are baking, or they will collapse.

Bake for 30 minutes. Turn the oven down to 350°F (180°C) and bake for another 25 minutes. Turn the oven off (again do not open it) and leave the puffs in for another 10 minutes, then remove from the oven and cool completely before filling. The puffs can be made ahead, wrapped airtight, and frozen for up to a month. They will lose their crispness, but 5 minutes on a baking sheet in a 400°F (200°C) oven will crisp them right up.

To finish the puffs, in a large bowl, whip the cream until it's very nearly stiff. Fold in the chilled crema al cioccolato until fully incorporated. Put the mixture into a pastry bag with a ½-inch (1.3 cm) round tip. You'll have to do this in a few batches. With a sharp paring knife, cut the top third of the puff off, and squeeze as much of the filling as you can into each puff. (There will be enough filling for ¾ cup/180 ml in each of the eight puffs.) Place the tops back on and dust with powdered sugar just before serving. The puffs can be made a few hours ahead of time and kept covered in the fridge, but they will soften.

lemon-anise pastries for easter and purim

PUPI CU L'OVA

◆◆◆

Makes 8

◆◆◆

All over the world, eggs are eaten as the symbol of rebirth, which rather goes against the idea of rebirth, given that that egg you just ate won't become a chicken. Sicilian kids get *pupi cu l'ova* (dolls with an egg) on Easter in the shapes of hearts, doves, baskets, and bells for girls, roosters for boys (let that last one sink in ...). They are more cookie than bread, but there is still something of a bread to them.

My nonna used to make these for the Jewish holiday of Purim, when they were known as *ojos de Haman*—eyes of Haman, the villain in the story of Purim. Here again is the Sicilian penchant for turning something awful into a pastry, at the same time commemorating it and neutralizing its awfulness.

½ cup (120 g) unsalted butter, at room temperature

¾ cup (150 g) sugar

½ teaspoon fine sea salt

2 eggs

¼ to ½ cup (60 to 120 ml) milk

1 tablespoon anise seeds

Grated zest of 1 lemon

1 teaspoon vanilla extract

4¾ cups (570 g) all-purpose flour, or 4¼ cups (500 g) 00 flour

1 teaspoon baking powder

8 small hardboiled eggs

Multicolored nonpareils

In a large bowl, mix the butter, sugar, and salt, stirring with a wooden spoon to combine well.

Break the eggs into a glass and beat them gently with a fork to combine. Add all but a couple of tablespoons of the egg to the butter mixture and mix. (Add 2 tablespoons of water to the remaining egg and set aside to use for egg wash later in the recipe.) Into the butter mixture, stir ¼ cup (60 ml) of the milk and the anise seeds, lemon zest, and vanilla extract. Sift the flour and baking powder together and add it to the bowl, mixing until the dough forms a ball. If the dough needs a little more moisture to come together, add up to ¼ cup (60 ml) of milk a little at a time. Turn the dough out onto a lightly floured surface and knead gently a few times. Don't overwork the dough. Wrap it in parchment paper or plastic wrap and chill for at least an hour and as long as a day.

Preheat the oven to 350°F (180°C). Line two baking sheets with parchment paper.

Divide the dough into eighths and roll each eighth ½ inch (1.3 cm) thick. With a sharp knife, cut out shapes—a dove, a bell, a basket, or a ring are all common. Save the scraps for the next step, but first, transfer the shapes carefully to the baking sheets. Brush all over with the reserved egg wash. Press a hardboiled egg, still in its shell, upright into the middle of each shape. Roll the dough scraps into 8-inch (20 cm) ropes and crisscross them over each egg, adhering it to its base.

If you'll be eating these right away, sprinkle generously with the nonpareils and bake for 30 to 35 minutes, or until the pupi are nicely browned. If you choose to make them ahead of time, don't add the nonpareils before baking. Cool completely and store airtight in the fridge for up to 2 days. When you're ready to eat them, brush the pupi with additional egg wash, sprinkle with nonpareils, and reheat at 350°F (180°C) for 15 minutes.

DOLCI DI BADIA

CONVENT SWEETS

Centuries-old tradition required that the day following their arrival the Salina family should visit the Convent of the Holy Spirit to pray at the tomb of Blessed Corbera, forebear of the Prince and foundress of the convent, who had endowed it, there lived a holy life, and there died a holy death.... The Prince liked the almond cakes the nuns made from an ancient recipe... and he was quite happy to pay over to the community a not inconsiderable portion of his own income, in accordance with the act of foundation.

—Giuseppe Tomasi di Lampedusa, *The Leopard*

◆◆◆

Palermo, September 2023

We are at the Monastero di Santa Caterina, having a private audience with Maria Oliveri, the culinary anthropologist who wrote the book *The Secrets of the Cloister: Stories and Recipes from the Monasteries of Palermo*. I Segreti del Chiostro is also the name of the pastry kitchen within the monastery, where for hundreds of years cloistered nuns created pastries and sweets destined for aristocratic tables. It has been preserved exactly as it was and is now open to the public, selling those same sweets according to recipes painstakingly collected by Ms. Oliveri. The nuns' recipes were closely guarded secrets and were transmitted orally, if at all, never written down. It must have been quite a job for Ms. Oliveri.

The Normans established the first monasteries in Sicily in the eleventh century, but it wasn't until the eighteenth century that they reached their greatest expression. In 1798, Palermo alone boasted thirty-nine monasteries and thirty-eight convents. Speaking of convents now, for purposes of this book and our talk of sweets, some were expressions of high spirituality, while others were simply institutions of redemption for orphans and women fallen from grace. Yet others were splendid retreats for daughters of noble houses, whose families heavily endowed convents for all but their firstborn girls, rather than depleting their riches and diluting their power with enormous dowries. It was in these last convents especially that Sicily's pastry arts flourished. There were the resources needed to purchase the very best ingredients; plenty of time in the nuns' monastic lives to devote to the art of pastry; and noble patrons eager to support—and even encourage—their efforts. Elaborate pastries became a status symbol among the aristocracy, evidence of the talents of the nuns and the wealth of the monasteries—and thus of the wealth of the families who endowed them.

Convents produced highly decorated Baroque masterpieces, cheekily called *peccati di gola*, or little sins of gluttony. With names like *fedde del cancelliere,* or chancellor's buttocks (pictured on page 122), *minne di vergine*, or virgin's breasts, and *trionfo di gola*, or triumph of gluttony, the pastries communicated the forbidden: lust, gluttony, resentment, and other unholy thoughts. Pastries, but not nuns, could teeter between the sacred and the profane.

With the unification of Italy in the late nineteenth century, feudalism collapsed, the landed aristocracy lost much of its land, the balance of power shifted from church to state, and a great number of monasteries and convents were seized and turned into public buildings or otherwise defunded.

Back at the *chiostro,* Ms. Oliveri is preparing a triumph of gluttony, two cassatas, six chancellor's buttocks, and three pairs of virgin's breasts for us to capture for this book. We photograph one of the cassatas (pictured on page 129) in one of the foundling wheels where babies were once abandoned, later used by the cloistered nuns to convey their sweets to the outside world. I ask her about the significance of the marzipan flowers decorating one of the cassatas. "Beauty," she says. "Only beauty." That may be the most meaningful symbol of all.

◆◆◆

IL TRIONFO DI GOLA

A TRIUMPH OF GLUTTONY

◆◆◆

A green hillock of pistachio jelly, of sweet ricotta and candied orange, of tiny raisins and morsels of chocolate; melting in the mouth like a cloud, carrying with it a perfume, intense and intoxicating; as though devouring a vast landscape, with all of its forests, its rivers, its meadows; a landscape made soft and delicate by a gossamer veil that contains and transforms it from a joy to the eyes to a joy of the tongue. It takes your breath away, this rare fragment of the sugared world, this most precious gift of the gods, dancing on your tongue.

—Dacia Maraini, *Bagheria*

Maraini goes on to say that, naturally, more than a teaspoonful of trionfo di gola is deathly cloying. I can attest to that. If you do want to make one, line a 2 quart (2 L) domed mixing bowl with plastic wrap that extends beyond the edges, then layer pan di Spagna (page 133) with *biancomangiare* (page 172), then more pan di Spagna, then crema di pistacchio (page 165), and more pan di Spagna, then *zuccata* (page 215), then crema di ricotta (page 164), and then more pan di Spagna, brushing each layer with Marsala or rum. You can sprinkle in chocolate bits or raisins plumped in Marsala, then cover the whole thing with plastic wrap. Refrigerate for at least one day. Meanwhile, make marzapane (page 62) and tint it with green food coloring.

Turn the cake over onto a serving platter and remove the bowl and plastic wrap. Roll out the marzapane and with it cover the whole triumphal thing, pressing the marzapane onto the sides to adhere. Decorate with sugar flowers, royal icing, gold dragees, and whatever else you desire, and serve immediately.

CAKES & Tarts

TORTE E CROSTATE

CASSATA

The origins of cassata can be traced back to the Arab domination of Sicily during the ninth to eleventh centuries. Cassata was, early on, a springtime cake traditionally made as an Easter specialty by the nuns in convents, or by Sicilian Jews for Purim. It was just pastry dough and unsweetened ricotta. The word cassata is believed to have derived from the Arabic *quas'at*, the name of the vessel in which it is prepared. But as Maria Oliveri—who runs I Segreti del Chiostro, the pastry shop at the Monastery of Santa Caterina in Palermo (which is now a museum)—cautions, this is all word of mouth. No definitive records exist.

Another early form of cassata had ricotta, sugar, and candied fruits all encased in a sweet pastry shell. The *gattò di ricotta*, a Jewish ricotta cake from Salemi, eschews the pastry crust in favor of breadcrumbs. Another type of cassata was made with goat's milk ricotta and was eaten by both Christian and Jewish Sicilians. They called it *cassati*.

Over time, the recipe for cassata evolved, incorporating more elaborate and luxurious ingredients. During the Spanish rule in Sicily, the cake began to feature marzipan, chocolate, and candied fruits, such as oranges and lemons, which became a signature element of cassata. At some point, I am told by Ms. Oliveri, a Palermo pastry chef by the name of Gullì began trafficking in cassata. But again, this is only hearsay. Cassata is a cake of many legends.

We do know that most cassatas were made in the convents and purchased by the aristocracy. In the eighteenth century, cassata underwent further transformations under the influence of the French. They introduced the use of pan di Spagna, or sponge cake, as the base for the cake. This addition gave cassata a lighter and more delicate texture.

During the nineteenth century, cassata became a popular dessert among the Sicilian aristocracy. It was often served at lavish banquets and on special occasions. The cake was adorned with intricate decorations, such as marzipan flowers, royal icing, and silver leaf, showcasing the skill and artistry of Sicilian pastry chefs and the nuns in convent kitchens.

In modern times, cassata has become a symbol of Sicily's culinary heritage as much as cannoli. Today's cassata is a *gattopardesque* masterpiece, which is to say worthy of the baroque tastes of Don Fabrizio of *The Leopard*—typically made with layers of sponge cake soaked in liqueur or sweetened syrup and filled with a creamy ricotta mixture flavored with flower essences, candied zuccata, and chocolate chips. The entire cake is then covered in green and white marzipan and sugar icing and decorated with candied fruits and baroque royal-icing flourishes.

cassata in the style of tiramisu

CASSATA FINTA

◆◆◆

Makes one 9-by 13-inch (23 by 33 cm) pan

◆◆◆

Cassata is not made at home, only in pastry shops and a few remaining convents, and for good reason: making one of these baroque masterpieces is more trouble than it's worth, unless you're a real baking enthusiast with a lot of patience and time on your hands. With all due respect to purists who will no doubt object, I therefore present to you the love child of a cassata and a tiramisu, which will give you all the flavors and textures of cassata. Your choice of garnishes allows as much baroque flourish as you're up for, with little of the fuss. My advice: Don't be timid. More is more here.

The ladyfingers used here are the crunchy ones typically used for making tiramisu and are widely available in international grocery stores and online, where they are also called *savoiardi*.

1 cup (240 ml) heavy cream

1 recipe crema al pistacchio (page 165)

Syrup

½ cup (100 g) sugar

½ cup (120 ml) water

½ cup (120 ml) rum or *elisir dei sette potenti* (page 27)

40 packaged ladyfingers (savoiardi)

1 recipe crema di ricotta (page 164)

Candied orange peel (page 210), chopped pistachios, chocolate bits, Amarena or Luxardo cherries, gold dragees, marzipan fruits, and/or royal-icing roses, for garnish

In a bowl, whip the cream to soft peaks and fold it into the pistachio cream.

To make the syrup, in a small saucepan, bring the sugar and water to a boil, stirring until the sugar is fully dissolved. Off the heat, stir in the rum. Transfer the syrup to a shallow bowl and allow it cool until it's lukewarm.

Set a 9- by 13-inch (23 by 33 cm) baking dish on the work surface. One at a time, dip the flat surface ladyfingers quickly in the syrup and then place them close together in the baking dish, creating a layer. Spread the ricotta cream evenly over the ladyfingers. Make another layer of ladyfingers dipped in syrup, and spread the pistachio cream evenly over that. Cover the dish and chill for at least 4 hours and up to a day.

Just before you serve the *cassata finta*, garnish it with your choice of candied orange peel, chopped pistachios, chocolate bits, cherries, gold dragees, marzipan fruits, flowers, or royal-icing roses.

sponge cake

PAN DI SPAGNA

◆◆◆

Makes two 9-inch (23 cm) round cakes

◆◆◆

Sponge cake is known as the "bread of Spain" in Sicily, and in Italy in general. Spanish sponge cake is made of egg yolks and whites beaten separately, but often, as here, the eggs are beaten whole, making it technically a genoise, or Genoese sponge cake. So which is it—Genoese or Spanish?

During the late Middle Ages, the Republic of Genoa, which had been a major maritime and commercial power in the Mediterranean and Black Seas, began putting its energy into banking. It was a close associate of imperial Spain, with Genoese bankers financing many of Spain's foreign initiatives (looking at you, Christopher Columbus). In 1749, the ambassador of the republic, the Marchese Pallavicini, was on a diplomatic mission to Spain. In order to curry favor with the king, the marchese asked his personal chef (who was, of course, part of his entourage) to make a special cake. The chef created a Genoese sponge with a few minor alterations intended to suit Spanish tastes and called it pan di Spagna in honor of the king.

Call it what you wish, it's now a building block of Sicilian baking, forming the base of the triumph of gluttony, the traditional cassata, and the *torta Savoia*. Baked in a single pan, it makes a fine "table" cake for any time of day.

6 eggs, at room temperature
¾ cup (150 g) sugar
Pinch of fine sea salt
1 teaspoon vanilla extract
1⅓ cups (150 g) cake flour
½ teaspoon baking powder

Cut circles of parchment paper to line the bottoms of two 9-inch (23 cm) round cake pans. Keep the sides unlined.

Place the eggs, sugar, salt, and vanilla extract in the bowl of a stand mixer. With the whisk attachment, whip at medium-high speed for 15 to 20 minutes, or until tripled in volume.

Meanwhile, preheat the oven to 350°F (180°C).

Sift the flour and baking powder together into a mixing bowl. With a large metal spoon or silicone spatula, fold a third of the flour, gently but with authority, into the egg and sugar mixture. Repeat this twice more with the remaining two-thirds of the flour. It's fine if a few lumps remain, so don't overmix.

Now divide the batter evenly between the two cake pans. Just before you put them in the oven, lift each pan 6 inches (15 cm) above the work surface and let it drop; this is to burst any large air bubbles and prevent the cakes from collapsing.

Bake for 40 to 45 minutes, or until the cake is evenly browned and bounces back when you lightly tap the top.

Cool completely, then run a knife around the inside edges of the pans to release the cakes and wrap them airtight until ready to use. Use within 2 days, or freeze for up to a month.

ricotta cheesecake for passover

GATTÒ DI RICOTTA

Makes one 8-inch (20 cm) cake

Here's my version of the *gattò di ricotta* from Salemi (see page 128). I've used matzo meal instead of breadcrumbs, so it makes a very nice dessert for Passover, when leavened bread is forbidden, or for any time you like.

1 tablespoon softened unsalted butter

3 tablespoons matzo meal, matzo cake meal, or breadcrumbs

1 pound (450 g) whole-milk ricotta, drained for 30 minutes

4 ounces (125 g) unflavored fresh goat cheese

1 cup (200 g) sugar

Grated zest of half a lemon and 1 mandarin

2 teaspoons orange-blossom water

1 teaspoon vanilla extract

½ teaspoon fine sea salt

4 eggs

3 egg yolks

Preheat the oven to 350°F (180°C).

Rub the inside of an 8-inch (20 cm) springform pan all over with the softened butter. Coat with the matzo meal or breadcrumbs. Wrap the outside of the pan in aluminum foil to prevent leaking.

Push the ricotta and goat cheese through a wire-mesh strainer with a silicone spatula into a large bowl. Whisk in the sugar, zests, orange-blossom water, vanilla, and salt. Then whisk in the eggs and the yolks, one at a time, mixing well after each addition. Scrape the batter into the prepared pan and place the pan into a larger, ovenproof pan. Pour boiling water into the larger pan and bake for 45 to 50 minutes, or until the top springs back when you touch it lightly. Turn off the oven and let the gattò cool, with the oven door closed, for an hour. Transfer to the fridge, cover, and cool completely. Remove the gattò from the pan before serving.

sweet pastry dough

PASTA FROLLA

◆◆◆

Makes enough for one 9- or 10-inch (23 or 25 cm) tart, plus a few scraps

◆◆◆

Another building block of Sicilian baking, pasta frolla is a sweet shortcrust pastry that's used for tarts, pastries, and filled cookies. I use part all-purpose or 00 flour and part *semola rimacinata*, or fine semolina flour (see page 21), for a bit more texture. This combination also makes the pastry a lovely, buttery gold color. Whenever my nonna made this, she'd bake up the scraps of dough and sprinkle them with cinnamon and sugar as a cook's treat for her granddaughter's hands.

1 cup (240 g) unsalted butter, at room temperature

¾ cup (150 g) sugar

½ teaspoon fine sea salt

1 egg

2 egg yolks

⅓ cup (80 ml) unflavored fresh milk

2¼ cups (270 g) all-purpose flour, or 2 cups (250 g) 00 flour

1⅔ cups (250 g) semola rimacinata (fine semolina flour)

In a large bowl, combine the butter, sugar, and salt, and stir until well combined. Stir in the egg, the egg yolks, and the milk, then the flours, all at once. Do not overmix; you want the dough to come together with no floury bits remaining.

Turn the dough out onto a lightly floured surface and knead it gently a few times. Divide the dough in half and wrap each half in parchment paper or plastic wrap. Refrigerate for up to 3 days, or freeze for up to a month.

baked ricotta and tart cherry torte

CASSATA AL FORNO

◆◆◆

Makes one 9-inch (23 cm) torte

◆◆◆

Made in the same shape as cassata, this is the rustic predecessor of that ornate and *gattopardesque* confection. There is another, fancier version of *cassata al forno*, shaped like a crown with glacé cherries standing in for jewels. That one is fashioned after a crown of Costanza d'Aragona, the queen consort of Frederick II in thirteenth-century Sicily. The actual crown rests in the museum of the cathedral in Monreale in Palermo; Costanza rests beneath it.

1 pound (450 g) whole-milk ricotta cheese

¾ cup (150 g) granulated sugar

Grated zest of half a lemon

1 sachet vanillina (see page 23) or 1 teaspoon vanilla extract

1 egg

1 recipe pasta frolla (page 135)

½ cup (80 g) pitted sour cherries in syrup, drained

Powdered sugar, to finish

The day before you plan to make this, place the ricotta in a strainer lined with paper towels or cheesecloth and let it drain in the fridge for at least 2 hours and up to 8.

Preheat the oven to 375°F (190°F). Have ready a deep 9-inch (23 cm) pie dish.

In a large bowl, combine the drained ricotta, sugar, lemon zest, vanillina, and egg. Whisk well to combine.

On a lightly floured surface, roll out half of the pasta frolla dough to an 11-inch (28 cm) disk. Carefully wrap the dough around the rolling pin and drape it over the pie dish. Press it gently into the bottom and up along the sides. Scrape the ricotta filling into the dish and top the filling with the cherries.

Roll out the other half of the dough, moisten the edges of the dough that is in the pie dish with a little water, and lay the just-rolled dough on top of the dish, pressing to make sure it adheres to the edges of the bottom crust. Bake for 25 to 30 minutes, or until the crust is well browned. Let it cool for an hour in the pie dish, then invert it onto a serving dish. Dust the top of the cassata al forno with powdered sugar before serving.

This will keep, covered, in the fridge for up to a week.

rustic tart at your whim

CROSTATA CAPRICCIOSA

◆◆◆

Makes one 9- or 10-inch (23 or 25 cm) tart

◆◆◆

This isn't especially Sicilian: you'll find *crostata* all over Italy. Most often it's made with whatever fruit preserves you happen to have on hand, but you could just as well fill it with crema pasticcera (page 165), crema al cioccolato (page 166), or crema di ricotta (page 164). It's not the sort of thing you fuss over, and if you don't want to go to the trouble of rolling out the dough, just press it into the pan with your fingers. Nobody will know. It's rustic, and that's its charm.

1 recipe pasta frolla (page 135)

1 tablespoon softened unsalted butter, for greasing the pan

1½ cups (510 g) crema al cioccolato (page 166), crema di ricotta (page 164), crema pasticcera (page 165), confettura di pesche (page 200), or best-quality fruit preserves

1 egg, for egg wash

When you make the pasta frolla, divide and wrap two-thirds and one-third of the dough separately. If your pasta frolla is freshly made, chill it for an hour before you use it. If you've made it ahead of time, take it out of the fridge 20 minutes before you plan to use it.

Preheat the oven to 400°F (200°C). With the butter, grease the sides of either a 9- or 10-inch (23 or 25 cm) tart pan with a removable bottom, or the same size springform pan.

On a lightly floured surface, roll out two-thirds of the dough to an 11-inch (28 cm) disk. Carefully wrap the dough around the rolling pin and drape it over the prepared pan. Press it gently into the bottom and up the sides of the pan.

Spoon the filling onto the dough in the pan and spread it evenly.

Make a lattice top the easy way: Divide the remaining dough into sixths and roll each piece into a 10-inch (25 cm) rope with your hands. Lay three ropes equidistant apart across the tart in one direction, and do the same with the other three ropes, laying them across the tart in the opposite direction. Press the ropes down lightly onto the edges of the tart to adhere. Trim off any overhanging dough.

Beat the egg in a small bowl with a fork until it starts to become foamy. Brush this onto the dough. Bake on a lower rack for 10 minutes, then lower the oven to 350°F (180°C) and continue to bake for another 40 to 45 minutes, or until the crust is nicely browned and the filling is bubbly. Cool completely before removing from the pan.

The crostata, if made with preserves, can be kept covered at room temperature for up to a week. If it has a milk-based filling, refrigerate it, wrapped airtight, for up to 3 days.

lemon bergamot olive oil cake

TORTA ALL'OLIO DI OLIVA, LIMONE, E BERGAMOTTO

Makes one 9-inch (23 cm) cake

This is a "table cake"—a simple, not overly sweet, one-layer cake that sits on the table (dining table or kitchen table or wherever the family eats), waiting for someone to slice a piece off for breakfast or a snack, or in case someone drops by for coffee.

I generally don't seek out olive oil cakes because they can so easily be—and so often are—greasy and tasting somehow like salad. But I like the idea of them. This is not a traditional Sicilian cake, but table cake is becoming a thing in Sicily as it is elsewhere, and I wanted to include one in this book that I myself would want to eat. It wasn't an easy or quick process. I knew I wanted it to have a citrus flavor to complement the olive oil, but I did not want the cake to taste like everyone else's. Around the same time, I was making liqueur with fresh bay leaves, and there is a cookie I found called *mastazzoli di riesi* that is said to be baked "under bay leaves." I haven't had any luck finding anyone who knows exactly what that means, but it gave me the idea to bake this cake *atop* bay leaves.

The pure bergamot extract that came by mistake instead of the jasmine extract I'd ordered turned out to be—dare I say?—a miracle. Bergamot is a citrus fruit that gives Earl Grey tea its flavor. It's got the sort of perfumy quality that's so typical of Sicilian sweets, and it plays well with lemon, even improving it. And the bay leaves? I knew they would give up their aromatic oils in service to the cake, and they did. They lend a botanical note that moves the olive oil in a new direction, far away from salad. I tried multiple ideas to include the bay leaves in ways that wouldn't require them to be removed before eating, but none worked as well as lining the bottom of the pan with them. The flavor is something special, and the bay leaves make such a lovely design when the cake is turned out of its pan. Isn't it to be expected that a bay leaf be removed before eating? You wouldn't eat it in a stew. It won't kill you if you do eat it, but it's better if you don't.

CONTINUED NEXT PAGE

Fati

2 tablespoons softened unsalted butter, for the pan

2 tablespoons sugar, for the pan

8 unsprayed fresh bay leaves

Cake

1¼ cups (250 g) sugar

1¼ cups (300 ml) extra-virgin olive oil

3 eggs

½ cup (120 ml) milk or yogurt

¼ cup (60 ml) freshly squeezed lemon juice, or half lemon juice and half bergamot juice

Grated zest of 1 lemon and 1 bergamot, or of 2 lemons

1 teaspoon pure bergamot extract

½ teaspoon fine sea salt

2 cups (240 g) cake flour

½ teaspoon baking powder

½ teaspoon baking soda

Preheat the oven to 325°F (160°C). Line the bottom of a 9-inch (23 cm) round cake pan with parchment paper. Now grease the bottom and sides of the pan with butter and sprinkle the butter with sugar to coat. Arrange the bay leaves, right side down, in the pan.

In a large bowl with a wire whisk, whisk the sugar into the olive oil a little at a time. Add the eggs one at a time, whisking as you go. Now whisk in the milk, juice, zest, extract, and salt.

Sift together the flour, baking powder, and baking soda and add this to the oil mixture in thirds, whisking after each addition. Scrape the batter carefully into the prepared pan so as not to dislodge the bay leaves and bake for 40 to 50 minutes, or until the cake is nicely browned and firm when you touch it lightly in the middle.

Cool the cake for 10 minutes, then turn it out of the pan onto a serving plate. It will keep, covered, at cool room temperature for up to a week.

mandarin-pistachio ring cake

CIAMBELLA AL MANDARINO E PISTACCHIO

◆◆◆
Makes one 10-inch (25 cm) ring or Bundt cake
◆◆◆

Sicilians eat cake and cookies and ice cream for breakfast. What's not to love about that? This is a table cake that's especially suited for breakfast, since it's made with whole raw mandarins—kind of like having your juice in solid form. If there's any cake left over, it gets better and moister as it sits, and it is just as good with tea in the afternoon. You could use any type of mandarin or tangerine, Satsuma, or Minneola for this, as long as they total one pound.

2 tablespoons softened unsalted butter, for the pan

2 tablespoons sugar, for the pan

Cake

1 pound (450 g) mandarins (about 4)

½ cup (120 ml) extra-virgin olive oil

1 cup (200 g) sugar

½ teaspoon fiori di Sicilia (see page 23) or vanilla extract

½ teaspoon fine sea salt

3 eggs

1 cup (100 g) pistachio flour (see page 21)

1 cup (120 g) all-purpose flour, or 1 cup (120 g) 00 flour

½ teaspoon baking powder

¼ teaspoon baking soda

Preheat the oven to 350°F (180°C). Grease a 10-inch (25 cm) tube pan or a ring mold with butter and sprinkle with sugar to coat.

To make the cake, cut the mandarins into quarters, peels and all. Remove and discard the stem nubbin and seeds. Puree until smooth in a food processor or blender, then set aside.

In a large bowl, whisk together the oil, sugar, fiori di Sicilia, and salt. Add the eggs one at a time, whisking as you go; then stir in the pistachio flour. In a separate bowl, sift together the all-purpose flour, baking powder, and baking soda and add this slowly to the large bowl, continuing to mix until all the flour is incorporated.

Now scrape the batter into the prepared pan and bake for 45 to 55 minutes, or until the cake is nicely browned and fragrant and the top is firm when you touch it lightly.

Cool for 10 minutes, then remove from the pan and transfer to a serving plate. The cake will keep, covered, at cool room temperature for up to a week.

apple and thyme honey cake with toasted fennel and almonds

TORTA MELE-MIELE

◆◆◆

Makes one 8-inch (20 cm) round cake

◆◆◆

If you mistakenly set your car's GPS to avoid major highways on your way to, let's say, the Catania airport from Modica, you will find yourself driving high up into the Monti Iblei, the Hyblaean Mountains. There, growing spontaneously through craggy rock formations, is wild—and very ancient—thyme. For centuries, Sicilian black bees have fed on its nectar to make the prized and highly aromatic *miele di timo*, or Sicilian thyme honey. Colony collapse, climate change, wildfires, and even certain agricultural innovations have destroyed much of this wild herb, threatening the survival of the black bees and making miele di timo increasingly rare. Greek thyme honey is a good substitute and is widely available in health food stores and in Greek and international groceries.

As you careen down those narrow mountain roads in late summer, masses of wild fennel, leggy and dry and beginning to go to seed, grow tall and insistent at the borders of the road. The *strade provinciali* are so narrow up there that you can reach your hand out the window and grab crowns of dry fennel flowers, loaded with seeds. Many varieties of heirloom apples, brought to Sicily by the Normans in the eleventh century, thrive in the high altitudes around Mount Etna. That four-and-a-half-hour detour, and the wholemeal croissants with dried wild herbs and honey at the Caffè Sicilia in Noto, inspired the creation of this cake. It gets moister and more flavorful as it sits, which so far, in my home, has never been more than two days.

½ cup (113 g) unsalted butter, softened, plus more for the pan

1 teaspoon fennel seeds

2 medium tart apples, such as Granny Smith

½ cup (125 g) miele di timo (thyme honey)

¼ cup (50 g) sugar

Grated zest of 1 lemon

2 eggs

½ teaspoon fine sea salt

½ teaspoon ground coriander

1 cup (120 g) all-purpose flour, or ½ cup plus 2 tablespoons (73 g) 00 flour

½ cup (50 g) almond flour

2 teaspoons baking powder

¼ cup (60 ml) milk

Preheat the oven to 350°F (180°C). Grease an 8-inch (20 cm) springform pan with butter.

Toast the fennel seeds in a small skillet over medium heat, stirring, until they begin to pop and become fragrant. Transfer to a plate and cool, then crush them with a mortar and pestle or in a spice grinder.

Peel, core, and slice the apples about ¼ inch (6 mm) thick. You should have 2 cups. Set aside.

In the bowl of a stand mixer, beat the butter with the honey, sugar, and lemon zest until light. Beat in the eggs one at a time, mixing well after each addition. Stir in the salt, crushed fennel seeds, and coriander.

In a separate bowl, combine the all-purpose flour, almond flour, and baking powder. Add half the dry ingredients to the egg mixture, then half of the milk, stirring after each addition. Repeat with the remaining dry ingredients and milk. Stir in the apples and scrape the batter into the prepared pan. Bake for 50 to 55 minutes, until the cake is nicely browned and fragrant and the top springs back when you touch it lightly. Cool in the pan for 5 minutes, then remove the springform and cool completely.

The cake will keep at room temperature for 3 days. After that, store tightly wrapped in the fridge for up to a week.

chocolate hazelnut layer cake

TORTA SAVOIA

◆◆◆

Makes one 9-inch (23 cm) cake

◆◆◆

This is a cake you'll find in pasticcerie throughout Sicily. Even though it's generally the only chocolate cake you'll see, for some reason it is always identified by the word *Savoia* written in icing on top. *Torta Savoia* is said to have been created in honor of the Duke of Savoy, to celebrate the unification of Italy and the Kingdom of Sicily in 1861, with hazelnuts from Piemonte—the seat of the House of Savoy—together with chocolate from Sicily. This is a bit fussy, but so was the unification.

½ cup (100 g) sugar

½ cup (120 ml) brewed espresso

Buttercream

¾ cup (180 g) unsalted butter, at room temperature, divided

4 ounces (115 g) milk chocolate, chopped

½ cup (135 g) Nutella

½ recipe crema pasticcera (page 165), chilled

Glaze

11½ ounces (330 g) dark chocolate, chopped

¼ cup (60 ml) canola oil

1 recipe pan di Spagna (page 133)

Dissolve the sugar in the espresso to make a syrup, and set aside until you're ready to assemble the cake.

To make the buttercream, place half of the butter and all of the milk chocolate in a heatproof bowl set on top of a saucepan of simmering water; stir as the chocolate melts. As soon as it does, remove the pan from the heat and whisk in first the Nutella and then the rest of the butter. Transfer it to a larger bowl and set aside to cool completely. When cool, whip the chocolate mixture with an electric mixer until it's light and fluffy. Gradually add the crema pasticcera, whipping all the while. Continue to whip, scraping the sides of the bowl with a silicone spatula as needed, until the buttercream is light and fluffy. Set this aside.

To make the glaze, melt the dark chocolate in a heatproof bowl set on top of a saucepan of simmering water, stirring as it melts. As soon as it does, whisk in the oil until the mixture is smooth and glossy. This will become firm as it cools; if necessary, just reheat it gently over simmering water until it liquefies.

To assemble the torta, slice both pan di Spagna cakes in half crosswise so you have four very thin layers. Place the first layer on the plate you intend it to stay on. Brush the top with some of the espresso syrup. Spread one-fourth of the buttercream evenly on the top of the first layer. Continue this operation until all the cake layers are used. Spread the last of the buttercream on the top and the sides of the cake in a thin layer. It won't entirely cover the cake; it's what's called a crumb coat, and it will prevent any stray crumbs from escaping into the glaze. Chill the cake, loosely covered, until the crumb coat is hardened, at least 30 minutes or up to a day.

To finish assembling the cake, have a long offset spatula ready. Put about ¼ cup (60 ml) of the glaze in a pastry bag with a small round tip for writing, or in a zipper storage bag with a tiny bit of the corner snipped off, or, if you happen to have a small plastic squeeze bottle, that's the easiest. Just pour the glaze in and snip off the very top.

Pour the remaining glaze onto the top of the cake and, with the spatula, coax it over the edges. Spread and smooth it onto the sides of the cake to completely cover the crumb coat. With the reserved glaze, write the word Savoia across the top and, if you like, add some fanciful squiggles, like Sicilian pastry cooks do.

YEASTED & *Fried*

L IEVMIATAF EEFRRTETLE

sweet rice fritters

ARANCINE DOLCI

◆◆◆

Makes 12

◆◆◆

Please don't call this a rice ball. These plump little spheres of deliciousness are called *arancine*, after the "little oranges" they resemble. You almost can't walk down a street in Palermo without meeting one, most often savory, filled with either a meat ragù, peas, and mozzarella; or ham, cheese, and béchamel (*arancine al burro*). In Catania and on the eastern side of the island, there are sweet rice fritters shaped like fingers. So why not a version somewhere in between? These *arancine dolci* hit all the notes: crunchy, creamy, aromatic, sweet, hot, cool, and a little bit chewy in the right way. The payoff is the soft, molten center of orange-blossom–scented pastry cream. You could opt to fill them with fruit preserves or Nutella with equal success. In any case, start these early in the day (or the day before) you plan to serve them.

Filling

¾ cup (170 g) crema pasticcera (page 165)

1 to 2 teaspoons orange-blossom water

Rice

¼ cup (60 g) unsalted butter

2½ cups (500 g) Arborio or Carnaroli rice

3¾ cups (900 ml) milk, divided

½ cup (100 g) granulated sugar

1 cinnamon stick

Half of a vanilla bean, split lengthwise

Grated zest of 1 orange

½ teaspoon fine sea salt

1¼ cups (150 g) fine dried breadcrumbs

¾ cup (100 g) all-purpose flour, or ⅔ cup (80 g) 00 flour

¾ cup (180 ml) water

1 egg

Canola, sunflower, or other neutral oil for deep-frying

¼ cup (30 g) powdered sugar, to serve

First, make the crema pasticcera, stirring in the orange-blossom water at the end. Cover and chill completely in the fridge, up to 2 days.

In a wide, shallow saucepan, melt the butter over medium heat. Add the rice and stir, cooking until it begins to turn opaque, about 3 minutes. Stir in 1 cup (240 ml) of the milk and continue cooking and stirring until the milk is almost completely absorbed. Add the remaining milk and stir in the sugar, cinnamon stick, vanilla bean, orange zest, and salt; bring to a boil. Turn down the heat, cover, and simmer for about 20 minutes, or until all of the liquid is absorbed. Spread the cooked rice out onto a baking sheet and let it cool. Cover and refrigerate until completely cooled, at least 4 hours or overnight.

When you're ready to finish the arancine, set up your assembly station. Prepare a small bowl of cold water for your hands. Put the breadcrumbs in a large shallow bowl. In another bowl, whisk the flour, water, and egg together. Set a baking sheet near the bowls. Line another baking sheet with paper towels or a metal rack and set it next to the stove. Pour 4 inches (10 cm) of oil into a deep heavy-bottomed pot.

Remove the chilled rice from the fridge and take out the cinnamon stick and vanilla bean. Divide the rice into 12 portions. To form the arancine, dip your hands in the water and grab a portion of rice in one hand. Flatten it out in the palm of your hand as much as you can. Cup your hand to make the rice curve into a well and fill this with a tablespoon of the pastry cream. Gather the rice up and pinch it together to enclose the pastry cream. Press and roll the rice in your hands to make a compact ball. Set aside on the unlined baking sheet while you roll the rest of the arancine.

Heat the oil to 350°F (180°C). In the absence of a deep-fry thermometer, test the oil by inserting the handle of a wooden spoon into it. If bubbles form quickly along the handle, the oil is ready for frying.

Dip one of the balls of rice into the flour mixture and let the excess fall back into the bowl. Roll it in breadcrumbs and lower it into the oil. Do the same with the rest of the rice balls, frying no more than 5 at a time. Fry until the arancine are nice and browned, about 4 minutes.

Remove them from the oil and drain on the paper towel–lined baking sheet or the rack. Dust arancine with powdered sugar just before serving.

sweet yeast buns

BRIOCHE COL TUPPO

◆◆◆

Makes 9

◆◆◆

If you've ever seen a French *brioche à tête*, the Sicilian *brioche col tuppo* will look familiar. But that's where the similarities end. The Sicilian brioche is less eggy than the French one, fragrant from a bit of citrus zest, and structurally sound enough to stand up to the icy granita that is its frequent companion. There's nothing better for breakfast on a scorching summer day in Sicily than a freshly baked brioche col tuppo, either filled with icy almond or lemon granita, or accompanied by a bowl of one or the other. You begin by plucking off the tuppo and dipping it in the granita, scooping some up on the way to your mouth. I love tearing off the last chunk and soaking up the puddle of granita at the end.

Brioche col tuppo is said to have been invented by the Normans, those frenchified Vikings who seized Sicily from the Saracens in the eleventh century. The word *tuppo* is Sicilian dialect for a low chignon that Sicilian women wore during the period of Norman rule. In the Norman tongue, it was called *toupin,* and in Gallic *toupeau*, words related to the modern French *toupet*, or lock of hair, and *toupée*, a wonky hairpiece for middle-aged men.

Sponge

½ cup (120 ml) milk, at body temperature (neither hot nor cold to the touch)

2 tablespoons sugar

2 teaspoons active dry yeast

1 cup (120 g) all-purpose flour, or ¾ cup (100 g) 00 flour

Dough

3 eggs

½ cup (120 ml) milk

½ cup (100 g) sugar

1 tablespoon honey

1 sachet vanillina (see page 23), or 1 teaspoon vanilla extract

Grated zest of 1 orange

Grated zest of 1 lemon

1 teaspoon fine sea salt

3⅔ cups (440 g) all-purpose flour, or 3⅓ cups (400 g) 00 flour, divided, plus extra for the work surface

Seed oil, such as canola or sunflower, for the bowl

⅔ cup (80 g) unsalted butter, at room temperature

First, make the sponge. In a medium bowl, stir together the milk, sugar, and yeast. Set this aside until it begins to get foamy, about 10 minutes. Stir in the flour, then cover the bowl and set aside for 1 hour to rise.

To make the dough, scrape the risen sponge into a large bowl. Break the eggs into a large glass and stir with a fork to combine. Pour all but a couple of tablespoons of the egg into the sponge, then cover the glass and refrigerate the reserved egg until the brioche is ready to bake (you'll use it for egg wash). Stir the milk into the sponge, then add the sugar, honey, vanillina, zests, and salt and stir until smooth. Now add 3 cups (360 g) of the flour (or a few tablespoons less if you're using 00 flour) and stir until it all comes together in a soft dough. Set the remaining measured flour aside to add during kneading if necessary.

Dust a work surface with a bit of extra flour. Transfer the dough to the surface and knead it gently but with authority, adding more flour bit by bit if it sticks. Don't push the dough into the board or it *will* stick. Just guide it across and over, gently but firmly. Keep kneading for 8 to 10 minutes, until the dough is smooth and feels soft, "like an earlobe" (says my nonna). Wash out the large mixing bowl, dry it, and rub the inside with a bit of oil. Put the dough back in and turn it over so its surface is coated with oil. Cover the bowl and let the dough rise until it's doubled in size, about 2 hours at room temperature or overnight in the fridge.

Dust the work surface with a few more tablespoons of flour. Turn the risen dough out onto the surface and with your fingertips (palms are too warm and will melt the butter) or a wooden spoon, work in the butter bit by bit until fully incorporated. Return the dough to the bowl, cover, and continue to let the dough rise until doubled in size, another hour or so.

Line two baking sheets with parchment paper and have ready a pastry brush. Take the reserved egg out of the fridge and stir in 2 tablespoons of water to make an egg wash.

Turn the dough out onto the work surface and divide it into 9 equal portions. Cut off about a quarter of each portion to form the tuppos. Roll each of the larger pieces into a smooth ball and place them on the baking sheets, three finger-widths from each other and from the pans' edges. With your finger, make an indentation in the center of each ball, all the way to the bottom, and push the dough away from the middle to leave about an inch (2.5 cm) open in the center. Brush this opening with egg wash to give the smaller pieces something to stick to. Roll the smaller pieces into smooth balls and pinch one end into a point. Insert the small balls into the centers of the large ones, pointy side down. Let rise in a warm place until doubled in size, about 1 hour.

Preheat the oven to 350°F (180°C).

Brush the surface of the buns gently but thoroughly with some of the remaining egg wash; bake for 15 minutes. Slide the pans out of the oven and carefully and quickly brush egg wash on the areas that have risen and so aren't covered with egg wash. Return the pans to the oven for another 10 to 15 minutes, until the brioches are nicely browned and shiny.

The brioche will keep for 2 days wrapped airtight at room temperature.

ricotta-filled donuts

IRIS

◆◆◆

Makes 8

◆◆◆

Per la cronaca—for the record—these are pronounced "EEreese," whether you order one or several, which you will want to do once you try them. The big difference between *iris* and, say, *bomboloni,* or mainland Italian donuts, is that iris get a coating of breadcrumbs before they're fried (or before they're baked, because iris take kindly to that too). The breadcrumbs give a whole bonus layer of pleasure to eating them: the crunchy contrast to the warm, pillowy dough giving way to the creamy center.

Iris were first made for the premiere, in 1901, of Pietro Mascagni's lyric opera *Iris.* Palermo pastry chef Antonio Lo Verso was so taken with the work that he created these in its honor.

I've given instructions for both baking and frying, but I think iris are at their best when fried. (Isn't everything?)

1 cup (230 g) whole-milk ricotta

Dough

½ cup (120 ml) milk, at body temperature (neither hot nor cold to the touch)

¼ cup (50 g) granulated sugar

2 teaspoons active dry yeast

2 cups (250 g) 0 (Manitoba) flour (see page 21) or bread flour

¼ cup (60 g) unsalted butter, at room temperature

½ teaspoon fine sea salt

Oil, for the bowl

Before you start making the dough, line a strainer with a paper coffee filter, paper towels, or cheesecloth. Put the ricotta you will use for the filling in the strainer over a bowl and refrigerate while you make the dough.

To make the dough, in a small bowl, stir together the milk, granulated sugar, and yeast. Set aside until the mixture begins to get foamy, about 10 minutes. Transfer to a large bowl and, with a wooden spoon, stir in the flour, butter, and salt until the dough comes together in a ball.

Turn the dough out onto a lightly floured board and knead it for a good 8 to 10 minutes, until it's smooth. Wash out the bowl, dry it, and rub with a bit of oil. Put the dough back in and turn it over so the surface is coated with oil. Cover the bowl and let the dough rise until it's doubled in size, about 2 hours at room temperature or overnight in the fridge.

Meanwhile, make the filling. In a small bowl, mix the drained ricotta, granulated sugar, and fiori di Sicilia. Stir in the chocolate. Cover and chill until you are ready to assemble the iris. The filling can be made up to a day in advance.

When the dough has risen, line two baking sheets with parchment paper. Turn the dough out onto a lightly floured surface, punch it down to release the air, and divide it into 8 equal portions (10 if you like them smaller). Form each portion into a ball by cupping your hand tightly over it and rolling it around and around on the work surface, putting a bit of pressure on it as you roll; it doesn't need to be perfectly shaped. Transfer the balls to the lined baking sheets as you finish them. Wet two light cotton towels, wring them out, and drape them over the baking

CONTINUED NEXT PAGE

Filling

⅓ cup (70 g) granulated sugar

½ teaspoon fiori di Sicilia, (see page 23), or 1 teaspoon vanilla extract

2 tablespoons chopped chocolate or chocolate chips

2½ cups (300 g) fine dried breadcrumbs

Canola, sunflower, or other neutral oil, for deep-frying (optional)

¼ cup (30 g) powdered sugar

sheets. Set aside for 30 minutes to rest before you fill them.

One at a time, flatten the balls as thinly as you can leaving the centers a bit thicker. Put a spoonful of the filling in the center of each dough circle and bring the edges up to meet in the middle to make a kind of pouch, enclosing the filling. Pinch the edges to seal it well and place the filled dough ball seam side down on one of the baking sheets. Repeat, leaving three finger-widths between each. Cover the baking sheets with plastic wrap and let the dough balls rise for another 30 minutes, or until doubled.

Fill a bowl with warm water and place the breadcrumbs on a small rimmed baking sheet or in a pie pan.

If you are going to fry the iris, pour 4 inches (10 cm) of oil into a heavy saucepan, place over medium heat, and heat to 325°F (160°C). In the absence of a deep-fry thermometer, test the oil by inserting the handle of a wooden spoon into it. If bubbles form quickly against the handle, the oil is ready for frying.

If you are going to bake the iris, heat the oven to 325°F (160°C).

As the oil or the oven heats, gently dip each dough ball into the warm water and roll it in the breadcrumbs to coat, letting the excess crumbs fall back into their pan. Flatten each ball slightly and return it to its baking sheet. When they are all formed, bake or fry the iris.

To bake, slide the baking sheets into the oven and bake for 25 to 30 minutes, or until the iris are well browned and the breadcrumbs are crunchy. Dust with powdered sugar just before serving.

To fry, lower one or two iris at a time into the hot oil, being careful not to crowd the pan. Fry for about 4 minutes on each side until they are well browned and the breadcrumbs are crunchy. Drain on paper towels or a wire rack placed on a baking sheet. Dust with powdered sugar just before serving.

sweet chickpea turnovers

CASSATEDDE PARTINICO

Makes 9

In the province of Palermo, and especially in the town of Partinico, you'll find these half-moon–shaped pastries in homes and pastry shops for Saint Joseph's Day—which, by the way, is also Father's Day—every March 19. Hot and crispy on the outside, *cassatedde* are filled with pureed chickpeas sweetened with honey, cinnamon, and chocolate. They aren't as strange as they may sound; prepared this way, chickpeas take on a flavor and texture reminiscent of glacé chestnuts. The effect is complete with a dusting of powdered sugar.

Dough

2½ cups (300 g) all-purpose flour, or 2 cups (240 g) 00 flour

3 tablespoons granulated sugar

¼ teaspoon fine sea salt

Grated zest of 1 lemon or 1 orange

¼ cup (60 g) cold unsalted butter, chopped

2 eggs

2 to 3 tablespoons Marsala or orange juice

Filling

3 cups (510 g) cooked chickpeas, or two 15-ounce (425 g) cans, drained and rinsed

⅔ cup (130 g) granulated sugar

3 tablespoons honey

1 teaspoon cinnamon

3¾ ounces (110 g) dark chocolate, chopped, or 3 ounces (85 g) mini chocolate chips

1 egg, for egg wash

Canola, sunflower, or other neutral oil, for deep-frying

Powdered sugar, for dusting

To make the dough, in a large bowl, whisk together the flour, sugar, salt, and zest. Work the butter in with your fingertips (not your palms, they're too warm and will melt the butter) until the mixture is crumbly and the pieces are no bigger than a pea. Make a well in the center of the flour and add the eggs and 2 tablespoons of Marsala. Using a fork, gradually work the dry ingredients into the liquid ingredients, mixing in a circular motion to nudge the dry ingredients into the well. Continue mixing until the dry ingredients are fully incorporated and the dough comes together in a ball. If the dough needs a little more moisture to come together, add the other tablespoon of Marsala.

Transfer the dough to a lightly floured surface and knead it gently a few times. Wrap it in plastic wrap and chill it while you make the filling. The dough can be made up to 2 days ahead of time. Take it out of the fridge 20 minutes before you plan to use it.

Now make the filling. This first part is fiddly, but worth it. When you have drained the chickpeas, remove the skins from as many of them as you can or feel inclined to. This will make for a much smoother filling.

In a food processor, pulse the chickpeas, sugar, honey, and cinnamon until smooth. Transfer this mixture to a bowl and stir in the chocolate.

With a fork, whisk together the egg and 1 tablespoon of water in a glass to make an egg wash. Line two baking sheets with parchment paper and dust the paper with a bit of flour.

To assemble the cassatedde, on a lightly floured surface, roll out the dough ⅛ inch (3 mm) thick. Punch out rounds with a 4-inch (10 cm) cookie cutter. (Don't reroll the scraps; fry them and dust them with cinnamon sugar for a snack.) Brush the dough rounds with egg wash and place a spoonful of filling in the center of each one. Fold in half and press the edges to adhere. You can press the edges with a fork or a pastry crimper too, just to make sure they are well sealed. Transfer the cassatedde to the baking sheets as you go.

Over medium heat, bring 4 inches (10 cm) of oil in a heavy saucepan to 350°F (180°C). In the absence of a deep-fry thermometer, test the oil by inserting the handle of a wooden spoon into it. If bubbles quickly form against the handle, the oil is ready for frying.

Carefully lower the cassatedde into the oil a few at a time. Do not crowd the pan. Fry for 2 or 3 minutes on each side, until puffed and nicely browned. Remove them from the oil and drain on paper towels or on a rack set over a baking sheet. Just before serving, dust them with powdered sugar.

ricotta-filled puffs for saint joseph's day

SFINCI DI SAN GIUSEPPE

Makes 14

True to the spirit of multi-culti Sicily, these are a French pastry with a Sicilian filling, an Arabic name, and a legacy tied to the Jews who once ran Sicily's thriving sugar industry. Nowadays, they spring up in pastry shops all over Sicily for Saint Joseph's Day, March 19, which is also, not coincidentally, Father's Day. In honor of dads, these delicate fritters, plump with sweetened ricotta cream or pastry cream, begin to show up in all of Sicily's pastry shops, often adorned with a cherry and a strip of candied orange peel. In Morocco, donuts resembling *sfinci* are commonly made for the Jewish holiday Hanukkah and are called *sfinj*. Sfinj came to Morocco with the Spanish Moors in probably the same way sfinci arrived in Sicily. These can be either baked or fried, depending on your pleasure. Both methods are presented here.

The Fried Ones

QUELLI FRITTI

Canola, sunflower, or other neutral oil (if frying)

1 recipe bignè dough (page 113)

1 recipe crema di ricotta with chocolate chips (page 164)

Powdered sugar, for dusting

14 strips candied orange peel (page 210), for garnish

14 glacé, Luxardo, or Amarena cherries, for garnish

In a deep, heavy saucepan over medium heat, heat 4 inches (10 cm) of oil to 325°F (160°C). In the absence of a deep-fry thermometer, test the oil by inserting the handle of a wooden spoon into it. If bubbles quickly form against the handle, the oil is ready for frying. Cut parchment paper into fourteen 3-inch (7.5 cm) squares. Fit a pastry bag with a 1-inch (2.5 cm) round tip and fill with the bignè dough. Pipe 2-inch (5 cm) mounds of dough onto each square and turn the square upside down into the oil. As the bignè puffs and cooks, you can pull the paper off with tongs and discard it. Fry sfinci until golden brown on one side, then turn over and fry on the other side, about 4 minutes total. Remove them from the oil with a slotted spoon and drain on paper towels or on a rack set over a baking sheet; allow to cool completely.

When cooled, split the tops of the sfinci in half with a sharp knife, leaving the bottoms intact. Pull the tops apart and fill generously with the ricotta cream, leaving the cream exposed in the center. Dust with powdered sugar and decorate the cream with a strip of orange peel and a cherry.

The Baked Ones

QUELLI AL FORNO

Preheat the oven to 400°F (200°C). Line two baking sheets with parchment paper.

Fit a pastry bag with a 1-inch (2.5 cm) round or star tip and fill with the bignè dough. Pipe 2-inch (5 cm) mounds of dough onto the baking sheets, leaving three finger-widths between each one and the edges of the pan. Flick a bit of water from your fingertips once or twice over the mounds and put the baking sheets in the oven. *Do not open the oven* while the puffs are baking. Bake for 40 minutes, then lower the oven to 325°F (160°C) for another 15 minutes. Turn off the oven but leave the sfinci in for a final 15 minutes. Remove from the oven and allow the sfinci to cool completely before filling.

When cooled, split the tops of the sfinci in half with a sharp knife, leaving the bottoms intact. Pull the tops apart and fill generously with the ricotta cream, leaving the cream exposed in the center. Dust with powdered sugar and decorate the cream with a strip of orange peel and a cherry.

lemon, raisin, and fennel seed fritters

FRITTELLE DI SAN MARTINO

◆◆◆

Makes
25 to 30

◆◆◆

November is usually a rainy month in Sicily, except during what's called Saint Martin's summer, a spell of warmth that arrives briefly and miraculously around November 11, Saint Martin's Day. Martin was a Roman soldier who became a saint for acts of generosity; one of which, it is said, caused God to make a shaft of bright sunlight cleave through the cloudy skies—and that, it is also said, is what causes a Saint Martin's summer. Saint Martin's Day is also an auspicious day to taste the new wine and eat sausages and roasted chestnuts to celebrate the harvest. (There's a proverb about overtaking a pig on Saint Martin's Day, but I'll spare you that here.) The real fun starts when the casks are open and the *novello*, or new wine, is tasted. The rather young-tasting wine is helped along by these *frittelle*, or fritters.

½ cup (75 g) golden raisins

¼ cup (60 ml) Marsala or orange juice

1 medium russet potato (about 9 ounces / 255 g)

1 cup (240 ml) milk

2 tablespoons honey

1 tablespoon active dry yeast

½ teaspoon fine sea salt

Grated zest of 1 lemon

2 teaspoons fennel seeds

2 cups (250 g) all-purpose flour, or 1¾ cups (210 g) 00 flour

Canola, sunflower, or other neutral oil, for deep-frying

Powdered or granulated sugar, for dusting

At least 1 hour and up to a day before you begin this dough, soak the raisins in the Marsala until most of the liquid is absorbed.

Peel the potato and cut it into quarters. Place it in a small saucepan and cover with water; the potato should be fully submerged. Bring the water to a boil, then turn the heat down, cover the pan, and simmer until the potato is tender, about 30 minutes. Drain the potato quarters and mash them or put them through a ricer, then allow them to cool.

In a small bowl, stir together the milk, honey, and yeast. Set this aside until it begins to get foamy, about 10 minutes. Transfer this mixture to a large bowl and, with a wooden spoon, stir in the cooled mashed potatoes, salt, zest, fennel seeds, and soaked raisins. Combine well. Now stir in the flour, a handful at a time, until a very soft dough forms. Lift the dough with your hand and slap it back down into the bowl with some authority. Do this another ten times, then cover the bowl and let the dough rise for about 2 hours, or until doubled.

In a heavy saucepan over medium heat, bring 4 inches (10 cm) of oil to 350°F (177°C). In the absence of a deep-fry thermometer, test the oil by inserting the handle of a wooden spoon into it. If bubbles quickly form against the handle, the oil is ready for frying.

Now grab two soup spoons. Dip both in the hot oil for a second, then scoop up a spoonful of dough with one and push it off the spoon into the oil with the other. Continue with more dough, but don't crowd the pan. Fry the frittelle until they are nicely browned on both sides, about 4 minutes total. They should turn over in the oil by themselves, but you may have to coax them. Remove them from the oil and drain on paper towels or on a rack set over a baking sheet. Put the sugar in a paper lunch bag and add the frittelle a few at a time. Close the bag and shake until they are coated with sugar. Serve warm.

A San Martino, ogni mosto diventa vino.
On Saint Martin's Day, all grape juice becomes wine.

SPOON SWEETS
& Fillings

DOLCI AL CUCCHIAIO

sweetened ricotta cream

CREMA DI RICOTTA

Makes about 2 cups (480 ml)

There's no Sicily without ricotta, and it would certainly mortify the whole culture of Sicilian dolci were ricotta to suddenly disappear. Ricotta cream is one of the backbones of Sicilian pastry, as a filling for cannoli, sfinci, cassata, iris, crostata, and more. Most often it's made with *ricotta di pecora*, or sheep's milk ricotta, except in the area around Ragusa, where cow's milk ricotta, *ricotta di mucca,* is common. To approximate the taste of Sicilian ricotta di pecora, mix 2 ounces (60 g) of unflavored fresh goat cheese to every 12 ounces (340 g) of cow's milk ricotta. If commercial ricotta is all you can find, look for one without emulsifiers or gelatin and drain it overnight in a strainer lined with a paper towel, a coffee filter, or cheesecloth.

1 pound (450 g) whole-milk ricotta

¾ cup (90 g) powdered sugar

¼ cup (60 g) unflavored fresh goat cheese (optional)

½ teaspoon cinnamon

¼ to ½ teaspoon fiori di Sicilia (see page 23), or 1 teaspoon vanilla extract

¼ teaspoon fine sea salt

¾ cup (180 ml) heavy cream

3 ounces (85 g) chopped chocolate or mini chocolate chips (about ½ cup; optional)

¼ cup (85 g) chopped candied orange peel (page 210) or candied watermelon rind (page 215) (optional)

Start this the day before you plan to serve it.

Line a strainer with cheesecloth, paper towels, or a paper coffee filter and place over a bowl. Place the ricotta in the strainer, cover with a plate, and chill for at least 2 hours and up to 8 hours.

Scrape the drained ricotta into a medium bowl and add the powdered sugar, goat cheese, cinnamon, fiori di Sicilia, and salt. In a separate bowl, whip the cream until it's billowy and nearly stiff. Fold it gently but with authority into the ricotta mixture. Fold in the chocolate and candied peel, if using.

Best used the day it's made or store airtight in the fridge up to a day.

sweetened pistachio cream

CREMA AL PISTACCHIO

◆◆◆

Makes
1¾ cup (240 ml)

◆◆◆

Somewhere between a ganache and a mousse, this pistachio cream is lusty, wicked, and moreish. If you're not a fan of white chocolate, don't let that put you off—we're using it here for its parts: sugar, fat, vanilla, and milk solids. Crema di pistacchio can fill anything that wants to be filled—bignè (page 113), iris (page 154), cannoli (page 106), sfinci, (page 158), a spoon ....

¾ cup (180 ml) heavy cream

4 ounces (115 g) chopped best-quality white chocolate

2 tablespoons pasta di pistacchio (page 212)

Start this several hours before you plan to use it.

In a small saucepan over medium heat, bring the heavy cream just to a boil. Off the heat, immediately add the white chocolate and set aside for 5 minutes to allow the chocolate to melt.

Whisk until smooth, then whisk in the pasta di pistacchio. Scrape the mixture into a bowl, cool to room temperature, then chill for at least 4 hours and up to 12.

When you are ready to use the pistachio cream, whip the mixture with an electric mixer until it's billowy and nearly stiff.

pastry cream

CREMA PASTICCERA

◆◆◆

Makes about
2½ cups (600 ml)

◆◆◆

Crema pasticcera is Sicilian pastry cream, along the same lines as *crème pâtissière*. It seems to have been brought to Sicily by the *monsù,* fancy French chefs employed in the kitchens of the aristocracy in the late eighteenth century. Colloquially, it's called *crema gialla,* since its golden yellow tint comes from the nice dark-orange yolks of the uncaged, aerobicized Sicilian chicken. Also colloquially, yolks are called *rossi*—red. Whatever can be filled, can be filled with crema pasticcera.

½ cup (100 g) sugar

⅓ cup (40 g) cornstarch

¼ teaspoon fine sea salt

6 egg yolks

1 sachet vanillina (see page 23), or 1 teaspoon vanilla extract

2 cups (480 ml) milk, divided

2 tablespoons (30 g) cold unsalted butter, chopped into pieces

In a heavy saucepan, whisk together the sugar, cornstarch, and salt. In a small bowl, whisk together the yolks and vanillina. Whisk half of the milk into the cornstarch mixture and half into the yolk mixture.

Place the saucepan over medium heat and cook the cornstarch mixture, whisking constantly, until it thickens and becomes glossy, about 2 minutes. Take the pan off the heat and slowly add the yolk/milk mixture, whisking constantly. Return the pan to the heat and continue whisking just until the mixture is thickened and smooth. Remove from the heat and immediately add the cold butter and whisk until completely incorporated. Scrape the crema into a bowl and place a round of parchment paper or plastic wrap directly on the surface to prevent a skin from forming (I don't do this, because the skin's my favorite part!), and chill completely before using. It lasts up to 2 days in the fridge.

chocolate custard filling

CREMA AL CIOCCOLATO

◆◆◆

Makes about 2½ cups (560 g)

◆◆◆

Have you noticed that the Italian word for chocolate seems to have a rather fluid gender identity? Sometimes you see it as masculine *cioccolato*, and other times it's feminine *cioccolata*.

You'll be understood either way, but I'm told that the masculine form is for solid chocolate and the feminine is for liquid. If you order cioccolata in a restaurant, you may get a chocolate beverage, while cioccolato will get you a *tavoletta*—a chocolate bar.

Crema al cioccolato is neither liquid nor solid. It's a thick eggless custard, but it lacks nothing in richness. Serve crema al cioccolato by itself in little cups with unsweetened whipped cream—a sort of Sicilian chocolate pudding—or use it as a filling, topping, or spread. Folded into softly whipped cream, it takes on a lovely mousse-like texture. I've used it to fill testa di turco (page 116).

½ cup (100 g) sugar

3 tablespoons unsweetened cocoa

¼ cup (40 g) cornstarch

1½ cups (360 ml) milk

¾ cup (125 g) finely chopped dark chocolate or chocolate chips

In a saucepan, whisk together the sugar, cocoa, and cornstarch. Add the milk gradually, whisking until smooth.

Now place the saucepan over medium heat and cook the mixture, whisking constantly, until it bubbles, thickens, and becomes glossy, about 5 minutes. Off the heat, immediately add the chocolate and whisk gently until the chocolate is melted and the mixture is smooth. Scrape into a small bowl, place a round of parchment paper or plastic wrap directly on the surface to prevent a skin from forming (I don't do this, because the skin's my favorite part!), and chill completely before using. Keeps in the fridge for up to a week, covered.

watermelon pudding

GELO DI MELONE

◆◆◆

Makes about 4 cups (960 ml)

◆◆◆

In the ninth century, shortly after the Saracens landed at Mazara del Valle to begin their conquest of Sicily, this dessert appeared. This "fool the eye" pudding was crafted using sugar, jasmine, pistachios, and the juice from the watermelon the Saracens brought with them, thickened with the wheat starch that was already there. Over time it evolved, taking in chocolate and *zuccata,* preserves made with the squash that arrived with the Spanish conquest in the sixteenth century. Nowadays, it's a typical summer treat, and during the rowdy August celebration of Palermo's patron saint, Santa Rosalia, *gelo di melone* is sold from kiosks, shops, and carts all over Palermo. For a modern meta-melon experience, garnish this with candied watermelon rind made in the style of zuccata (page 215).

One 5-pound (2.25 kg) watermelon

½ cup (100 g) sugar

½ cup (60 g) cornstarch

Chopped chocolate, candied watermelon rind (page 215), cinnamon, and/or jasmine blossoms, to garnish

Peel and seed the watermelon and cut it into chunks. In a blender, puree the chunks in batches, then strain in a wire-mesh sieve over a bowl, pressing on the fruit to get every little bit of juice. Measure out 4 cups (960 ml) of the watermelon juice. You can discard the pulp and enjoy any leftover juice. Have ready four 1-cup (240 ml) ramekins, custard cups, teacups, or dessert bowls.

In a large saucepan off the heat, whisk together the sugar and cornstarch, then gradually whisk in the juice until the mixture is smooth. Now turn the heat to medium and cook, whisking constantly, until the mixture is thickened and clear, about 4 minutes.

If you'd like to unmold the gelo to serve, spritz the interiors of the dishes you're using as molds with a little water, then fill with the gelo. Cool to room temperature, then cover the dishes with plastic wrap and chill completely in the fridge. They should unmold without fuss, but if not, just dip the molds briefly in a larger bowl of very hot—but not boiling—water, give them a little shake and turn out onto plates; or serve straight from the molds. Garnish with any combination of chocolate bits, candied watermelon rind, cinnamon, or jasmine blossoms.

the melon and mint one

QUELLO DI MELONE PURCEDDU E MENTA

◆◆◆

Makes about 4 cups (960 ml)

◆◆◆

In Sicilian dialect, "little piggie" is the endearing nickname given to Purceddu melons—not for their flavor, but for their portly oval shape. Their rinds are wrinkly and dark green; it almost goes without saying that their pale flesh is syrupy sweet and aromatic. What makes Purceddu special is that they are ... durable. Traditionally laid out on terraces or hung from balconies, they've been known to last past Christmas! They make a delicate, elegant gelo. Any sweet white- or green-fleshed melon can be substituted.

One 5-pound (2.25 kg) Purceddu or any other sweet white- or green-fleshed melon

8 fresh mint leaves, plus more for garnish

⅓ cup (70 g) sugar

½ cup (60 g) cornstarch

Peel and seed the melon and cut it into chunks. Puree in a blender with the mint leaves, then strain, pressing on the fruit to get every little bit of juice, and measure out 4 cups (960 ml) of juice. Anything extra is the cook's treat. Have ready four 1-cup (240 ml) ramekins, custard cups, teacups, or dessert bowls.

In a large saucepan, whisk together the sugar and cornstarch, then gradually whisk in the juice until the mixture is smooth. Now place the saucepan over medium heat and cook, whisking constantly, until the mixture is thickened and clear, about 4 minutes. If you'd like to unmold the gelo to serve, spritz the interiors of the dishes you're using as molds with a little water, then fill with the gelo. Cool to room temperature, then cover the dishes with plastic wrap and chill completely in the fridge. They should unmold without fuss, but if not, just dip the molds briefly in a larger bowl of very hot—but not boiling—water, give them a little shake, and turn out onto plates; or serve straight from the bowls. Garnish with mint leaves.

MELONI SICILIA
Bonta' e Sapori di Sicilia
Di Benedetto Giovanni
Il meglio dell'Uva di Mazzarrone
Frutta di Bronte
GIRASOLE
UVA DI MAZZARRONE
GIOVANNI AULINO

the pomegranate and orange one

QUELLO CON MELOGRANO E ARANCIA

◆◆◆

Makes about 4 cups (960 ml)

◆◆◆

Pomegranate is the symbol of Persephone and also of Sicily—but surprisingly, Sicilians don't seem to lust after them as they do after other fruits. But I do. So here you go—a gelo, fit for the goddess of the underworld.

½ cup (100 g) sugar

½ cup (60 g) cornstarch

3 cups (720 ml) pomegranate juice

1 cup (240 ml) freshly squeezed orange juice

Pomegranate seeds, for garnish

Have ready four 1-cup (240 ml) ramekins, custard cups, teacups, or dessert bowls.

In a large saucepan, whisk together the sugar and cornstarch, then gradually whisk in the pomegranate and orange juices until the mixture is smooth.

Now place the saucepan over medium heat and cook, whisking constantly, until the mixture is thickened and clear, about 4 minutes. If you'd like to unmold the gelo to serve, spritz the interiors of the dishes you're using as molds with a little water, then fill with the gelo. Cool to room temperature, then cover and chill completely in the fridge. They should unmold without fuss, but if not, just dip the molds briefly in a larger bowl of very hot—but not boiling—water, give them a shake, and turn out, or serve straight from the bowls. Garnish with pomegranate seeds.

almond-milk pudding with roasted apricots

BIANCOMANGIARE CON ALBICOCCHE ARROSTITE

Serves 4

If you like panna cotta, you'll appreciate *biancomangiare*. It's a delicate, supple little pudding of ancient Roman origin, made from freshly pressed almond milk. In the beginning, biancomangiare was made with lard, almonds, rice flour, and fish or pounded chicken breast. It's come a long way, baby.

Apricots give their all here: in addition to roasting the flesh to accompany the almond-milk pudding, you can save the kernels to help add a bitter-almond flair to your next batch of homemade almond milk (page 224). Nothing needs to be wasted. The recipe calls for heavy cream, but you can substitute more almond milk to keep it vegan.

Pudding

¾ cup (150 g) sugar

½ cup (80 g) cornstarch

¼ teaspoon fine sea salt

2 cups (480 ml) freshly made almond milk (page 224) or best-quality store-bought

1 cup (240 ml) heavy cream or more almond milk

1 teaspoon vanilla extract, or 1 sachet vanillina (see page 23)

1 to 2 teaspoons orange-blossom water

Roasted Apricots

Unsalted butter, for the pan

Juice of half a lemon

6 very ripe fresh apricots

¼ cup (50 g) sugar

In a large saucepan off the heat, whisk together the sugar, cornstarch, and salt, then gradually whisk in the almond milk, cream, vanilla, and orange-blossom water until the mixture is smooth. Have ready four 6-ounce (175 ml) ramekins, custard cups, teacups, or dessert bowls.

Now turn the heat to medium and cook the mixture, whisking constantly, until the mixture is thickened and clear, about 4 minutes. If you'd like to unmold these to serve, spritz the interiors of the dishes you're using as molds with a little water, then fill with the custard. Cool to room temperature, then cover with plastic wrap and chill in the fridge at least 4 hours and up to 24.

About half an hour before you plan to serve these, make the roasted apricots.

Preheat the oven to 350°F (180°C). Grease a glass or ceramic baking dish with a little butter.

Squeeze the lemon juice into a medium bowl. Cut the apricots in half, saving the kernels for almond milk (page 224) if you like, and cut each half in three. Transfer the apricots to the bowl with the lemon juice. Add the sugar, toss, and transfer to the prepared baking dish. Roast until the apricots soften and begin to caramelize, about 30 to 40 minutes.

Now unmold the puddings, which should happen without fuss. If not, just dip the molds briefly in a larger bowl of very hot—but not boiling—water, give them a little shake, and turn out; or serve straight from the bowls, accompanied by the roasted apricots and any juices left in the roasting pan.

benedictine chocolate pudding

GELO DI CIOCCOLATO

Serves 4

Among Sicily's eighteenth-century nobility, if you weren't first in the birth order, you would take your title but nothing else and live out your life in a monastery. It wasn't the worst thing that could happen; the monastery would receive generous endowments from your family, so your life, though relatively frugal, would have every appropriate comfort. Benedictine monasteries were especially favored by the nobility, and several still stand today. In Catania, Il Monastero di San Nicolò l'Arena is a spectacular example of a well-endowed eighteenth-century Benedictine monastery. It looks more like a *palazzo nobile* than a place of piety and worship.

The Benedictines, an order of *buongustai,* or gourmands, concocted liqueurs and cooked meals as lavish as was permitted within the rules of the order. I used to have a little book of Benedictine recipes from San Nicolò that I bought in Catania. In it, there are strict sumptuary laws prescribed by the abbot, emphasizing *assolutamente* the avoidance of excessive food.

A journal recovered from the monastery in 1988 laid out the austere—relatively—pescatarian menu for Holy Thursday in 1790.

FIRST COURSE	**Fish**
SECOND COURSE	**Soup, bread, anchovies, asparagus, more fish, and lentils**
THIRD COURSE	**Still more fish (swordfish pie, sea bass), more asparagus, fennel, and broccoli**
FOURTH COURSE	**Beans with raisins and chestnuts**
FIFTH COURSE	**Gelo di cioccolato**

Here is a recipe for the Benedictine *gelo di cioccolato* that the monks enjoyed that day in 1790. I received it many years ago from the Ruta family of Antica Dolceria Bonajuto in Modica, where, with almost religious fervor, the Rutas devote themselves to preserving the history of Modican chocolate. They make the gelo with water, the way the monks did, but I prefer milk. I've made a few embellishments on the original recipe to make it luscious, creamy, and a bit less austere.

3½ ounces (100 g) chocolate from Modica (see page 100), or 1 round tablet Ibarra Mexican chocolate

3 cups (720 ml) cold milk (dairy or plant), divided

⅓ cup (50 g) cornstarch

¼ cup (50 g) sugar

Pinch of fine sea salt

1 teaspoon vanilla extract

Chop the chocolate and combine it with 2 cups (480 ml) of the milk in a large saucepan. Over medium heat, melt the chocolate slowly in the milk, stirring often.

In a large bowl, stir together the cornstarch, sugar, and salt. Whisk in the remaining 1 cup (240 ml) of cold milk. Now add the chocolate milk from the saucepan a little at a time, whisking constantly until it's fully incorporated and no lumps remain. Return the mixture to the saucepan and cook over medium heat for 4 minutes, whisking constantly, until thickened and glossy. Whisk in the vanilla. Have ready four 6-ounce (180 ml) ramekins, custard cups, teacups, or dessert bowls to use as molds.

If you'd like to unmold the gelo to serve, spritz the interiors of the molds with a little water before filling with the pudding. Cool to room temperature, then cover and chill completely before serving. They should unmold without fuss, but if not, just dip the molds briefly in a larger bowl of very hot—but not boiling—water, give them a shake, and turn out. Or serve straight from the bowls.

FROZEN *Sweets*

GELATI E GRANITE

SELTZ
LIMONE
SALE

lemon ice scented with lemon leaves

GRANITA AL LIMONE

Makes 1 quart (1 L)

Lemon ice is lemon ice, and it's perfect in its simplicity. But consider the leaves: they've got just as much flavor as the fruit, but in a greener, more herbaceous way. In Sicily, you'll see them threaded on skewers with meat or vegetables for the grill, where they release their lovely herby oils into the food. So why not put them to work here, adding an herbal note to the lemoniness of the granita? If you happen to know a nice unsprayed lemon tree and have access to its leaves, try this. If not, use grated lemon zest instead.

I love eating this lemon granita in a tall glass with a splash of seltzer and a sprinkling of sea salt. It's a twist on one of my favorite hot-weather beverages in Sicily, *seltz con limone*, which is freshly squeezed lemon juice, seltzer water, and sea salt. It's the most thirst-quenching drink for a hot Sicilian day.

3 cups (720 ml) water

1 cup (200 g) sugar

8 large unsprayed lemon leaves, crushed in your hands to release the oils, or the grated zest of 2 lemons

1 cup (240 ml) freshly squeezed lemon juice, from 8 lemons (Meyer lemons, if you can get them)

In a large saucepan, combine the water and sugar. Drop the crushed lemon leaves into the pan (or add the zest). Over medium-high heat, bring to a boil, then turn the heat down and boil gently for a good 5 minutes. Whisk in the lemon juice, remove from the heat, cover loosely, and let cool to room temperature.

Strain the cooled mixture into a 2-quart (2 L) metal baking dish or cake pan; discard the leaves. Freeze for 1 hour until the mixture has begun to freeze around the edges. With a fork, stir and mash the frozen granita, combining it with the unfrozen part. Do this again 30 minutes later, then every 15 minutes when it really starts freezing quickly. Depending on your freezer, it should take about 2½ hours for the granita to freeze fully, with a fine, flaky texture. Store airtight in the freezer for up to a month.

coffee and cardamom granita

GRANITA AL CAFFÈ TURCO

◆◆◆

Makes
1 quart (1 L)

◆◆◆

The scents of mothballs and seeds lingered around my great-grandmother. Cloves for sweet breath, fennel for digestion, cardamom for coffee. She was from the Dardanelles in Turkey, where, in the spirit of "the enemy of my enemy is my friend," the sultan had welcomed the Jews expelled from the territories of the Spanish crown in the fifteenth century, including Sicily. Among them, my family. Cardamom coffee is a Turkish thing, and it reminds me of the milky coffee my great-grandmother spilled into saucers "on accident," which as a small child I was permitted to sip.

Order a *mezza con panna*, especially around the province of Messina, and you'll get a glass filled with half coffee granita and half unsweetened whipped cream. "*Mashallah!*" ("Praise God!"), she would have said.

3 cups (720 ml) freshly brewed espresso or very strong coffee

1 cup (240 ml) water

1 cup (200 g) sugar

6 cardamom pods, crushed

¼ teaspoon fine sea salt

1 cup (240 ml) heavy cream

Measure the freshly brewed coffee into a large bowl.

In a small saucepan, bring the water, sugar, cardamom pods, and salt to a boil. Turn the heat down and boil gently for a good 5 minutes. Whisk this mixture into the brewed coffee, cover the bowl loosely, and let cool to room temperature.

Strain the cooled coffee mixture into a 2-quart (2 L) metal baking dish or cake pan; discard the cardamom pods. Freeze for 1 hour until the mixture has begun to freeze around the edges. With a fork, stir and mash the frozen granita, combining it with the unfrozen part. Do this again 30 minutes later, then every 15 minutes when it really starts freezing quickly. Depending on your freezer, it should take about 2½ hours for the granita to freeze fully, with a fine, flaky texture. Whip the heavy cream until stiff, and keep it in the fridge until ready to serve.

Serve the granita in glasses, topped with a thick lashing of whipped cream. Store airtight in the freezer for up to a month.

almond-milk cremolata

CREMOLATA ALLE MANDORLE

◆◆◆

Makes
1 quart (1 L)

◆◆◆

If you've been to the Caffè Sicilia in Noto, it's likely you've had your way with a warm brioche dipped into a bowl of slushy *granita di mandorle* made with freshly pressed almond milk. It's a deliciously fragrant contrast of textures and temperatures. Although they call it a granita, it's more like a *cremolata*. Unlike granita, where you want a bit of crunch, the ice crystals in cremolata are very tiny, making it smoother and creamier on your tongue than granita. It isn't solid, but cold and slushy.

The name cremolata is deceiving, giving the impression that there's cream in it, but here the word means "creamy." If you have an ice cream maker, by all means use it, but you can make this cremolata quite nicely this way. Just please make the almond milk from scratch; commercial almond milk doesn't have enough flavor or creaminess.

4 cups (1 L) almond milk (page 224), divided

1 cup (200 g) sugar

¼ teaspoon fine sea salt

¼ teaspoon pure almond extract (optional)

In a large saucepan, whisk together 1 cup (240 ml) of the almond milk, the sugar, and the salt. Bring the mixture to a boil over medium heat, then boil gently for 5 minutes, whisking to dissolve the sugar. Remove the pan from the heat and whisk in the remaining almond milk and the extract, if using.

Cover the pan loosely and let the mixture cool to room temperature. If you're using an ice cream maker, chill the mixture in the fridge, then proceed according to the directions for your ice cream maker.

Otherwise, pour the cooled mixture into a 2-quart (2 L) metal baking dish or cake pan. Freeze for 1 hour until the mixture has begun to freeze around the edges. With a fork, stir and mash the frozen part, combining it with the unfrozen part. Do this again 30 minutes later, then every 15 minutes when it really starts freezing quickly. Depending on your freezer, it should take about 2½ hours for the cremolata to freeze fully, with a fine, flaky texture.

For an extra-creamy texture, whir the frozen cremolata briefly in a food processor or high-speed blender just before serving. Serve in–or with–a brioche col tuppo (page 150).

Amor Fati

chocolate cremolata

CREMOLATA DI CIOCCOLATO

Makes
1 quart (1 L)

This is a duet of textures, with Modican chocolate adding a sugary crunch to the cool, creamy cremolata. If you can't find Modican chocolate, substitute Mexican chocolate—the sort that comes in thick disks and is used to make hot chocolate.

1 cup (200 g) sugar

¼ cup (30 g) unsweetened cocoa

¼ teaspoon fine sea salt

3 cups (750 ml) water

¾ cup (130 g) grated cold-processed dark chocolate (from Modica or Mexico)

1 teaspoon vanilla extract

In a large saucepan, whisk together the sugar, cocoa, and salt. Whisk in ½ cup (120 ml) of the water to make a smooth paste, then add the rest of the water and whisk to combine. Bring the mixture to a boil over medium heat, whisking constantly so the cocoa doesn't burn. Remove the pan from the heat and let the syrup cool for 10 minutes. Add half of the grated chocolate and the vanilla, and whisk until it's dissolved, then whisk in the rest. It's OK if bits of chocolate don't dissolve; they'll add a nice crunch to the finished cremolata.

Cover the pan loosely and let the mixture cool to room temperature. If you're using an ice cream maker, chill the mixture in the fridge, then proceed according to the directions for your ice cream maker.

Otherwise, pour the cooled mixture into a 2-quart (2 L) metal baking dish or cake pan. Freeze for 1 hour until the mixture has begun to freeze around the edges. With a fork, stir and mash the frozen part, combining it with the unfrozen part. Do this again 30 minutes later, then every 15 minutes when it really starts freezing quickly. Depending on your freezer, it should take about 2½ hours for the granita to freeze fully, with a fine, flaky texture.

For an extra-creamy texture, whir the frozen cremolata briefly in a food processor or high-speed blender just before serving. Serve in small glasses with lashings of very lightly sweetened whipped cream, if you like.

pistachio milk cremolata

CREMOLATA DI PISTACCHIO

Makes
1 quart (1 L)

After spending the morning with me at a very special pistachio orchard at the base of Mount Etna (read about I Lochi on page 27), the orchard's owner, Luigi, insisted we pay a visit to the Pasticceria F.lli Gangi in Bronte, where they use strictly Bronte pistachios, and only from his orchard, in all their sweets. He called ahead, and by the time we arrived, there was a cavalcade of pistachio-based pastries, drinks, gelati, and cremolata waiting for us. With the pistachios I brought back from Bronte, I created my rendition of their cremolata.

4 cups (1 L) pistachio milk (page 212), divided

¾ cup (150 g) sugar

2 tablespoons mild honey

¼ teaspoon fine sea salt

¼ teaspoon almond extract (optional)

In a large saucepan, whisk together 1 cup (240 ml) of the pistachio milk, the sugar, honey, and salt. Bring the mixture to a boil over medium heat, then boil gently for 5 minutes, whisking to dissolve the sugar. Remove the pan from the heat and whisk in the remaining pistachio milk and the almond extract, if using.

Cover the pan loosely and let the mixture cool to room temperature. If you're using an ice cream maker, chill the mixture in the fridge, then proceed according to the directions for your ice cream maker.

Otherwise, pour the cooled mixture into a 2-quart (2 L) metal baking dish or cake pan. Freeze for 1 hour until the mixture has begun to freeze around the edges. With a fork, stir and mash the frozen part, combining it with the unfrozen part. Do this again 30 minutes later, then every 15 minutes when it really starts freezing quickly. Depending on your freezer, it should take about 2½ hours for the cremolata to freeze fully, with a fine, flaky texture.

For an extra-creamy texture, whir the frozen cremolata briefly in a food processor or high-speed blender just before serving.

Serve in–or with–a brioche col tuppo (page 150), piled onto an ice cream cone, or in a glass with a spoon.

frozen chocolate and hazelnut praline cream

SEMIFREDDO AL CROCCANTE

◆◆◆

Makes one 9-by 5-inch (23 by 13 cm) loaf

◆◆◆

Just after culinary school, I went to work as an apprentice at a restaurant in Lugano owned by my Bianchi relatives. Lugano is about as far away from Sicily as you can get while still speaking Italian. (It is in fact the Italian canton of Switzerland.) I had read about their restaurant in *Gourmet* magazine and wrote to them. They were happy to welcome a new family member into the fold.

The food at Da Bianchi was very much the buttery, creamy, eggy food of the North, and *semifreddo* was a specialty. Semifreddo (meaning "semi-cold" is akin to a French parfait—a sort of unchurned ice cream made by folding whipped cream into a custard or meringue base and freezing it in a mold. Safe to say it was brought to Sicily by the *monsù*—those haute Parisian chefs employed by the Sicilian nobility of the eighteenth century, who trafficked in opulent, rigorously French cuisine.

The semifreddo in Lugano was made from a base of zabaglione, a foamy custard made by whipping egg yolks, sugar, and Marsala constantly over a bain-marie, or double boiler, until frothy and light. This was the domain of my elderly aunt, who would enter the kitchen once a day with perfectly manicured nails and measure the ingredients in eggshell units: each egg yolk takes half an eggshell of sugar and half an eggshell of Marsala. When she was done, she'd spoon off enough zabaglione for the semifreddo, hand it to the chef, and leave the rest for me and the other two apprentices, Franco and Marco, to eat over a scoop of ice cream as a treat, the ice cream melting under the warmth of the zabaglione.

When I returned to the U.S., I discovered from my uncle, the family genealogist, that those Bianchi weren't related to us at all. Bianchi is to Italy—especially the North—what Smith or Jones is to the U.S.!

Praline

1 cup (150 g) toasted hazelnuts

¾ cup (150 g) sugar

¼ cup (60 ml) water

2 tablespoons unsalted butter

1 tablespoon lemon juice

½ teaspoon fine sea salt

Zabaglione

6 egg yolks

⅔ cup (160 ml) coffee liqueur

Semifreddo

1⅔ cups (400 ml) heavy cream, divided

½ cup (85 g) chopped dark chocolate

1 teaspoon vanilla extract

To make the praline, preheat the oven to 300°F (150°C).

Rub a thin film of flavorless oil onto a rimmed baking sheet. Place the hazelnuts on another rimmed baking sheet and keep them warm in the preheated oven while you caramelize the sugar.

Have a candy thermometer ready near the stove. In a large, heavy saucepan over medium-low heat, stir together the sugar, water, butter, lemon juice and salt. Keep stirring with a wooden spoon until all the sugar is dissolved but the mixture isn't yet boiling. Remove the spoon and don't put it back in until I tell you to. Then turn up the heat to medium-high and boil, swirling the pan every now and then so the syrup cooks evenly. After about 10 minutes, the syrup will begin to turn brown and thicken. Now resume stirring with your wooden spoon until the mixture reaches 300°F (150°C) on the candy thermometer. Take the warm hazelnuts out of the oven and add them to the pan. Stir for a minute to coat them in the caramel, then carefully turn the praline out onto the prepared baking sheet in a thin layer. Let cool completely.

The praline can be made up to a few days ahead of time. Just wrap it airtight and store it at cool room temperature.

To make the zabaglione, set a heatproof bowl over a saucepan of simmering water. Add the yolks and liqueur to the bowl and whisk together. Keep whisking continuously for 6 to 8 minutes, until the mixture has thickened and holds its shape. Take the bowl off the heat and let the mixture cool to room temperature; then cover the bowl and chill the zabaglione until it's completely cold, at least 2 hours. Keep in the fridge until you're ready to make the semifreddo, no more than 8 hours or it will begin to lose volume.

To make the semifreddo, line a 9- by 5-inch (23 by 13 cm) loaf pan with plastic wrap that extends beyond the edges of the pan; set aside.

In a small saucepan over medium heat, bring ½ cup (120 ml) of the cream just to a boil. Remove the pan from the heat, add the chocolate, and whisk until the chocolate is melted, then whisk in another ½ cup (120 ml) of the cream. Chill this chocolate cream until completely cold, at least 30 minutes.

Meanwhile, break up the praline into shards; save a few for garnish, wrapped airtight. Pulse the rest in a food processor until ground to the texture of uncooked rice (or seal it in a strong plastic or silicone bag and smash it with a hammer).

In a large bowl, combine the remaining ⅔ cup (160 ml) of heavy cream, the chocolate cream, and the vanilla extract. Whip with an electric mixer until the mixture is billowy and holds its shape. By hand, gently fold in the zabaglione, then the praline. Scrape the mixture into the prepared loaf pan, cover tightly, and freeze for a good 12 hours. When you're ready, turn the semifreddo out of the loaf pan onto a serving plate and garnish with the reserved praline shards. Slice crosswise into 1½ inch (4 cm) servings.

◆◆◆

HOW TO ORDER Gelati IN SICILY

◆◆◆

Ordering gelati in Sicily is sometimes more a sport than a pastime. There is a way to do it that makes sense once you understand the rules.

1. Look for the cashier. This is your first stop. This person may not be anywhere near the gelati: hands that touch dirty money do not serve you food. Remember this.

2. Decide what you want before approaching the cashier. You will ask for either a *coppetta* (cup) or a *cono* (cone), then specify the size: *piccolo* (small), *medio* (medium), or *grande* (large). You can say *"Vorrei una coppetta piccola,"* and you'll get a small cup. Use the same sentence structure with the variations I just mentioned.

3. The cashier doesn't care what flavors or how many of them you want, so don't bother saying. Pay, take your *scontrino* (receipt), and head for the scoopers.

4. Now, how many flavors do you want? You can have two flavors (*due gusti*) in a small, three flavors (*tre gusti*) in a medium, and four flavors (*quattro gusti*) in a large. Don't try to customize beyond this. It's rude.

5. Sicilians don't queue up, so don't expect a tidy line. It may be chaotic, but just make eye contact with a scooper, draw their attention to your receipt without waving it maniacally, and be ready to tell them the flavors you want. They may look at your receipt and know what you've paid for, or they may ask you.

6. Would you like to taste before you choose? Say *"Posso avere un assaggio per favore?"* Don't ask for more than two. It's rude.

7. Do you want whipped cream? Say *"Con panna, per favore."*

THEN THERE'S

Granita

It can be served in a cup, in a brioche, or in a cup with a brioche alongside to dip into the granita. Here are your lines:

1.

"VORREI UNA GRANITA AL LIMONE (CON PANNA)"

will get you granita in a cup or glass with whipped cream on top (my favorite).

2.

Say

"VORREI UN BRIOCHE"

if you want a brioche.

3.

And if you're anywhere near Messina, make like a local and order a

"MEZZA CON PANNA,"

coffee granita with a lashing of whipped cream on top.

4.

FINAL NOTE

Never mention or compare gelato or granita that you've had in any other part of Italy. Just don't.

PRESERVES
& Candy

CONSERVE E CROCCANTI

blood orange and rose water marmalade

MARMELLATA DI ARANCE ROSSE E ROSE

◆◆◆

Makes six 8-ounce (250 ml) jars

◆◆◆

I'm suspicious of shortcuts. Something usually gets lost in the haste. But this marmalade method isn't a shortcut, it's an *efficiency*.

I realize that sometimes the lines I draw between what I will and won't do are squiggly and arbitrary. For example, I have no problem at all tending to orange peel for four days, lulling it slowly and gently into a candied state of sweet surrender; but for orange marmalade, I have no patience. None. Until I tasted some made by an elderly French woman named Jacqueline, who had better things to do than sweat over a pot for four days. It's a formula that can be scaled up or down, depending on how many oranges you have. You cut up the oranges, weigh them, then soak them in the same weight of water for twelve hours. Then add the same weight (of the oranges) of sugar and follow the directions below. I've done the weighing for you here, but the formula will hold if you scale it up. I'm giving traditional canning instructions here, but if you feel more comfortable, follow the directions for heat canning in any reputable manual. The U.S. Food and Drug Administration (FDA) also has directions on its website.

The *moro* or Moor orange is another passenger on Slow Food's Ark of Taste. It grows in eastern Sicily, in rich volcanic soil near Mount Etna. The moro has aromatic thin skin and deep red flesh. You can use any thin-skinned orange for this marmalade, but a blood orange is preferable. It has the right perfumed quality to play nicely with rose water.

1½ pounds (6 small or 680 g) blood oranges, or other small, thin-skinned oranges or mandarins

1½ pounds (3 cups or 720 ml) filtered water

1½ pounds (3⅓ cups or 680 g) sugar

2 tablespoons rose water

With a sharp knife, cut the oranges into quarters and remove and discard any seeds, the stem nubbin, and any loose bits of white pith. Slice the quarters as thinly as you can and add the slices to a bowl as you go. Add the water to the oranges in their bowl, cover loosely, and set aside at room temperature for 12 hours.

After 12 hours, transfer the oranges and water to a wide, shallow copper, stainless-steel, or enameled pot. Add the sugar to the pot, stirring with a wooden spoon. Place the pot over medium heat and stir until the sugar is dissolved. Boil gently, uncovered, for 1 hour, stirring once or twice.

Set your timer for another hour. Keep the mixture at a gentle boil but stir it more often. Meanwhile, boil or otherwise sterilize six 8-ounce (250 ml) canning jars and their lids and keep them hot.

During the third hour, keep vigil at the stove, stirring frequently, while the mixture simmers and thickens. Do not let it boil furiously, or the sugar will caramelize and make the marmalade bitter. After 45 minutes, start testing it with a candy thermometer. When the marmalade reaches 222°F (105°C), take it off the heat, stir in the rose water and immediately ladle it into the sterilized jars. Wipe off the jar rims with a wet cloth and screw on the lids, then quickly turn the jars upside down. Allow them to cool completely. Once they are cool, turn them upright: they are now vacuum sealed.

strawberry jam made with homemade pectin

CONFETTURA DI FRAGOLE

◆◆◆

Makes three 8-ounce (250 ml) jars

◆◆◆

While you are cooking the preserves, you'll need to sterilize three 8-ounce (240 ml) canning jars according to your preferred method. If you are not a veteran canner, follow the directions for heat canning in any reputable manual. The U.S. Food and Drug Administration (FDA) also has directions on its website.

1 quart (680 g) very ripe fresh strawberries

1½ cups (300 g) sugar

Juice of 1 lemon

1 cup (240 ml) homemade pectin (see page 203)

Rinse the berries and remove the green tops and inner white hulls with a sharp paring knife. Cut into quarters (you should have about 3 cups) and transfer them to a wide, shallow 4-quart (4 L) pot; stir in the sugar. Set aside, covered loosely with a tea towel, for an hour or two to allow the sugar to dissolve and begin to soak into the fruit. With a potato masher or large fork, crush the berries as finely as you wish.

Stir in the lemon juice and pectin. Over medium heat, bring the mixture to a boil, stirring with a wooden spoon until the sugar dissolves. Boil gently, stirring from time to time, for 30 minutes. Turn the heat down a bit if it starts boiling furiously. Continue cooking, stirring more frequently, for another hour or so, until the preserves have thickened and become glossy. Skim any foam that has come to the surface and pour into sterilized jars with lids.

Either can with your preferred canning method or simply turn the jars of hot jam upside down and leave to cool completely.

PESCA SPACCARELLA
€ 1,00 CHILO
PESCA MONTAGNOLA BIVONA
€ 2,00 CHILO
BANANE
1,50 CHILO
UVA ITALIA
2,00 CHILO
PERE
€ 1,50 CHILO
PRUGNE
€ 1,50 CHILO
PATATE
1,30 CHILO
LA P NA
Tel. 360

late-harvest sun-cooked peach preserves

CONFETTURA DI PESCHE SETTEMBRINE COTTE AL SOLE

◆◆◆

Makes three to four 8-ounce (250 ml) jars

◆◆◆

I generally don't like to mess with the perfection of voluptuous, sweet tree-ripened peaches any more than simply eating them over the kitchen sink to catch all the syrupy juices running down my chin. Sun-cooking is one of the very few exceptions. In warm climates, the late-summer sun is hot enough to concentrate the fruit's juices into a soft-set preserve while retaining their just-picked flavor. It's a slow process, but only requires a few minutes of hands-on tending a day and seems like the natural progression of what nature already started.

As I write this, it's late August, and in a week I'll be in Sicily, where I intend to buy a nice big basket of *pesche Settembrine*, or September peaches; some to abandon myself to in all their juicy stickiness and the rest to preserve in the heat of the sun. Sicily's Pesca Settembrina is a late-harvest variety grown in the town of Leonforte in the belly button of the island. It ripens in September and October and even into November. As the fruits begin to form, each one is wrapped in a paper bag to protect it from the early autumn wind and insects, harvested only when it's perfectly ripe. Any soft tree-ripened peach would work for this method.

When you have scraped the seeds out of the vanilla bean to use in this recipe, chop the bean and store it in a small bottle covered with vodka or rum. In forty days it will become vanilla extract.

Juice of 1 lemon

1½ pounds (680 g) very ripe peaches, about 4 medium peaches

¾ cup (150 g) sugar

Half of a vanilla bean, split lengthwise, and seeds scraped

Halve the lemon and squeeze its juice into a wide, shallow copper, enamel or stainless steel pot. Cut the peaches in half, remove the pits, and slice thinly. Add them to the pot and toss to coat with the lemon juice. Scrape the vanilla seeds into the sugar and stir the vanilla sugar into the peaches.

Cover the pot and let it sit for an hour, or until the peaches start giving up their juices.

Transfer the contents of the pot to a large, shallow stainless-steel pan or enameled tray and put it in full summer sun, covered loosely with a piece of net or cheesecloth. (Laugh if you want, but the dashboard of a closed car parked in full sun will do the trick nicely.) Every 4 or 5 hours, give the peaches a good stir and leave in full sunlight until the sun sets. Bring the pan inside at night (or leave it in the car if you're using the dashboard method) and take it back outside the next day. Continue with this operation until the preserves are thickened the way you like. Depending on the weather and your tastes, it could take anywhere from 3 days to 5. Store, refrigerated in sterilized jars up to 3 months, or in the freezer for up to 6 months.

sweet tomato and lemon leaf preserves

CONFETTURA DI POMODORI E FOGLIE DI LIMONE

◆◆◆

Makes four 8-ounce (250 ml) jars

◆◆◆

You may not think of tomatoes as a fruit, but that's just what they are.

Biting into a perfectly ripe high-summer tomato as I would a plum or peach, it occurred to me that such a fruit would make beautifully aromatic, luscious preserves. I was right, and this is the recipe I came up with. I've given it the typical Sicilian flavors of cinnamon and cloves, with lemon and lemon leaves to add some sharpness and keep the palate awake. I love it in a kind of breakfast bruschetta, dribbled on some good whole-milk ricotta atop a piece of toasted semolina bread, or alongside shards of salty cheese.

While you are cooking the preserves, you'll need to sterilize four 8-ounce (250 ml) canning jars according to your preferred method. If you are not a veteran canner, follow the directions for heat canning in any reputable manual. The U.S. Food and Drug Administration (FDA) also has directions on its website.

2 pounds (about 1 kg) super-ripe summer tomatoes (about 6 medium)

¾ cup (150 g) sugar

Juice of 1 lemon

A 1-inch (2.5 cm) piece of cinnamon stick

4 whole cloves

8 large unsprayed lemon leaves, crushed in your hand to release the oils, or large strips of zest from one fat lemon, removed with a vegetable peeler

Working over a strainer placed in a bowl, quarter the tomatoes, removing the seeds and letting them fall into the strainer. Cut off and discard the stem nubbins and chop the tomatoes coarsely; transfer to a wide, shallow copper, stainless-steel, or enameled pot.

Add any juice from the bowl to the pot along with the sugar, lemon juice, cinnamon stick, cloves, and lemon leaves. Cover and set aside for 1 hour, or until the tomatoes start giving up their juices.

Over medium heat, bring the mixture to a boil, stirring with a wooden spoon until the sugar dissolves. Boil gently, stirring from time to time, for 30 minutes. Turn the heat down a bit if it starts boiling furiously. Continue cooking, stirring more frequently, for another hour or so, until the preserves have thickened and become glossy. Fish out and discard the lemon leaves or zest, cinnamon stick, and cloves, and ladle the preserves into sterilized jars. Wipe the jar rims with a wet cloth and screw on the lids, then quickly turn the jars upside down. Allow them to cool completely. Once they are cool, turn them upright: they are now vacuum sealed. Store at room temperature for up to a year. Refrigerate once opened.

quince paste

COTOGNATA

◆◆◆

Makes sixteen 2-inch (5 cm) pieces

◆◆◆

Quince—*mele cotogna*—is a hard sell, no question. In fact, everything in and of the quince is hard: the skin, the raw flesh, the cores. But like a person whose charms only reveal themselves once you get to know them, a properly prepared quince becomes tender, submissive, and fragrant. *Mele* means "apple," and though quince resemble apples, they are actually closely related to cherries and almonds.

Cotognata is a sweetened quince paste made when quinces are fully ripe, in October and into early November. It is so identical to Spanish *membrillo* that it's safe to say the method arrived with the Spanish conquest of Sicily, even if the quince trees had been planted centuries before by the Greeks. Traditionally, the cooked paste is poured out either onto dinner plates to solidify, or into little ceramic molds with designs carved into them. You can find antique molds at the flea markets in Palermo and Catania or at my favorite antique shop, Nicolaci, in Noto or new ones made in Santo Stefano on Sicily's north coast. Here, I'm giving you the option of using a single square pan and then cutting the paste into squares or bars, or of using any little ceramic or silicone molds you have around. Homemade pectin is an optional side product of this recipe, and instructions for making it are woven into the method for the cotognata.

Cotognata pairs well with salty cheeses (pecorino is a favorite), is a lovely little sweet snack on its own, and makes a charming addition to a fresh fruit plate.

CONTINUED NEXT PAGE

4 medium quince (about 2 pounds; 1 kg)

Juice of 1 fat lemon

4½ cups (850 g) sugar

Scrub the quince, rinse them, and put them in a pot just large enough to fit them. Add water to cover by a couple of finger-widths. Boil over medium-high heat until the quince are tender and easily pierced with a fork, about 40 minutes. Remove the quince and set them aside until they're cool enough to handle. Reserve the water in its pot. When the quince are cool, peel them, then remove the core, seeds, and any woody bits and add these to the water in the pot for making pectin. Set the pot aside while you proceed with the cotognata.

Mash the cooked quince in a bowl with a fork; puree them in a food processor; or pass them through a food mill. Add the mashed or pureed quince to a wide shallow pot with the lemon juice and sugar. Have ready an 8-inch (20 cm) square pan or sixteen 2- to 3-ounce (60 to 90 ml) ceramic, metal, or silicone molds.

Bring the quince to a boil, turn the heat down to medium-low, and stir with a wooden spoon as the quince cooks down and thickens to a paste. It will take about an hour, so keep stirring and be patient. The quince will turn a dark ruby color and begin to get glossy. Turn the heat down to low if it begins to sputter and splash. Keep stirring. The cotognata is ready when it becomes glossy and comes away from the sides of the pan.

Preheat the oven to 175°F (80°C). Spritz the interior of the pan or the molds with water and scrape the cotognata into them. Level the top(s) with a spatula spritzed with water.

Bake the cotognata for 1½ hours. Better still, put the cotognata out in what's left of the late-summer sun for 2 days, uncovered, bringing it in at night. Cool to room temperature, turn out of the pan, and cut it into small squares or bars; or unmold. Cover loosely with a kitchen towel and set aside for a day or two to dry out a bit more. Store airtight at room temperature in a tin lined with dried bay leaves for up to a month, or in in the fridge for 3 months.

Once the cotognata is cooling in its molds, make the pectin if you so wish. Set the pot of quince water and trimmings over medium-high heat and simmer until the liquid turns a deep rosy color, reduces to about 2 cups (480 ml), and thickens. Strain it into jars and discard the solids. Store the jars in the fridge or freezer. Now you have homemade pectin that you can use to naturally thicken sauces or homemade jams.

sun-dried wine grape confection

MOSTARDA DI UVA

Serves 6 to 9, or more

Mostarda has nothing at all to do with mustard. *Mosto* refers to grape must, the freshly crushed juice of wine grapes that still contains the stems, seeds, and skins. Mostarda is a sweet made during the *vendemmia*, or wine harvest, with the first pressing of the grapes. When it's freshly made, you can eat it with a spoon like a pudding or, like cotognata (see page 203), you can pour it into molds to solidify and let it dry in the sun for a few days, when it takes on the texture of an elegant Sicilian gumdrop.

Don't let the ashes put you off. Wood ash is alkaline and is used to raise the pH of the wine grapes, turning acid to sugar and sweetening the juice naturally. I sometimes like to add a few soft dried figs at the end for depth of flavor and their chewy texture.

3 tablespoons wood ash, from burned grapevines or your local wood-burning-oven restaurant

2 quarts (2 L) freshly pressed grape juice, preferably from grapes destined to become wine, or from Concord grapes

1 cinnamon stick

¾ cup (90 g) cornstarch

6 dried figs, stemmed and chopped (optional)

¼ cup (30 g) chopped toasted almonds

First, sift the wood ash to remove any large bits.

Pour the juice into a large stainless-steel or enameled pot and add in the ashes and cinnamon stick; stir. Simmer over medium heat until reduced by half, about 30 minutes. Strain through a clean cotton pillowcase to remove all of the ash and the cinnamon. Do not press or squeeze the pillowcase, just let it strain in its own time. The juice will be perfectly clear. Allow it to cool completely.

Have ready two rimmed 9-inch (23 cm) dinner plates or six to nine 3-inch (7.5 cm) ceramic or silicone molds.

Rinse the pot, pour in about one-third of the cooled juice, and whisk in the cornstarch until it's fully incorporated and no lumps of dry starch remain. Whisk in the rest of the juice and stir in the chopped figs, if using. Slowly bring to a boil over medium heat. Cook and stir with a wooden spoon until the mixture thickens and becomes glossy and translucent, about 3 minutes, then cook 1 minute more. Remove from the heat.

Spritz the dinner plates or molds with water and immediately ladle the mostarda into them. Sprinkle with the chopped almonds and set aside to cool. You can eat it warm like a pudding or let it dry in the autumn sun for a couple of days: it will take on the consistency of a gumdrop. Then turn it out of the plates or molds and return it to the sun for another day. Keep in a tin lined with dried bay leaves, or airtight in the fridge for up to a month. In the photo (opposite), the mostarda on the left is freshly made, not dried in the sun; the lighter one on the right has been dried in the sun and stored in bay leaves.

candied orange peel

SCORZA D'ARANCIA CANDITA

◆◆◆

Makes 4 cups (about 300 g)

◆◆◆

If you plan to truly capture the essence of Sicilian pastry, you'll have to have the best-quality candied orange peel you can get your hands on—best bet: make it yourself. The process is admittedly a bit of a faff, but it is worth the effort. It takes four days, and there's no way around that. Don't believe anyone who says they have a quick and easy, shortcut method for this. It just takes time for every little cell in the peel to fully drink in the syrup and soften up.

My nonna would use this same method to candy kumquats, which were abundant in the Los Angeles of my childhood (and which to this day I do not love). After the process of candying them was complete, she would string them together on a cotton thread and hang them from the knob of a kitchen cabinet to dry until they were no longer sticky.

3 large unsprayed navel oranges

Pinch of fine sea salt

2 cups (400 g) sugar

2 cups (480 ml) water

Slice the top and bottom off each orange, just until you expose the flesh. Now score the oranges all around, top to bottom, making your cuts ½ inch (1.3 cm) apart. Pull the peels off in strips and save the flesh for another use.

Put the peels and salt in a pot with water to cover and bring to a boil over high heat. Boil 5 minutes, drain, and repeat this operation two more times, with fresh water each time. Remove the peels from the pot and set them aside.

Bring the sugar, water, and drained peels to a boil over medium heat, stirring to dissolve the sugar. Boil for 5 minutes, remove from the heat, and leave the peels in the syrup, covered and at room temperature, for at least 12 hours and up to 24. Repeat this operation for 3 more days, simmering the peels over medium heat in the same syrup and leaving the covered pot at room temperature for 12 to 24 hours. It will thicken more each day. On the final day, day 4 of the whole process, simmer gently, stirring, until most of the syrup is absorbed, about 30 minutes.

Rub a thin film of flavorless oil on a cooling rack set on top of a baking sheet. Remove the peels from the syrup and transfer to the rack to drain and dry until just tacky to the touch. This will take several hours and up to a day, depending on the humidity, after which you can store the peels airtight at room temperature. I like to roll them in sugar and let them dry again until no longer tacky, another day or so. Store them airtight at room temperature for up to 6 months.

pistachio butter

PASTA DI PISTACCHIO

◆◆◆

Makes 2½ cups (600 g)

◆◆◆

In Bronte, in the shadow of Mount Etna, where the finest of Sicily's pistachios grow, this is called Green Gold. *Pasta di pistacchio* is to peanut butter what diamonds are to plastic. Slathered onto a nice piece of toasted semolina bread and dribbled with orange-blossom honey or the blood orange marmalade on page 196, it makes the sexiest PB&J analog you're ever likely to taste.

1 pound (450 g) shelled roasted pistachios

¼ cup (60 ml) flavorless oil, such as canola

½ teaspoon fine sea salt

Get comfortable, this may take a bit. (Worth it!)

Place the pistachios, oil, and salt in a blender, and blend at high speed for 5 minutes, scraping down the sides of the blender as you go. Continue blending and scraping until the pistachios start to really break down and liquefy. It won't seem possible at first, but stick with it and it *will* happen. It could take a good 10 minutes; the longer you blend, the smoother it becomes. In the end, you'll have 2½ cups (600 g) of smooth liquid gold. Store it in the fridge for up to a month; it will thicken up considerably.

preserved watermelon rind in the style of zuccata

FINTA ZUCCATA CANDITA

◆◆◆

Makes three 8-ounce (250 ml) jars

◆◆◆

The *cucuzza* is a large, curly pale-green vegetable (technically a gourd, though it's called a squash), with little to recommend it. Once you get past the tough, inedible exterior, the flesh is dense and crisp (and flavorless). Somewhere along the line, a resourceful nun, likely faced with a glut of *cucuzze* growing in the cloister garden, set to candying them, simmering them slowly with sweet spices, lemon, and sugar. It is my opinion (not fervent enough to be a belief) that if you cooked a shoe slowly in enough sweet spices, lemon, and sugar, it wouldn't be half bad either. Anyway, candied cucuzza is called *zuccata,* and it shows itself as tiny palest-green cubes in many ricotta-based pastries and as thin strips curled into baroque swirls atop the fanciest of cassatas. In the right hands, it's something special.

However, even if you do find a cucuzza, making zuccata takes a lot of work; more than it's worth, in my opinion. I failed at it twice, ending up with tough, slimy little cubes of sugary nothing both times. The whole operation was like taking the time to craft an ornate frame for a so-so painting.

Not willing to give up on it, I racked my brain for something else to apply the same technique to—something dense and crisp with no character of its own—and the answer came to me in the form of a watermelon rind. Funny thing is, one of the garnishes I've seen on gelo di melone, or watermelon pudding, is zuccata, which is supposed to look like ... watermelon rind! Use only the white part of the rind, not the tough green outer part.

While you are cooking the rind, you'll need to sterilize three 8-ounce (250 ml) canning jars according to your preferred method. If you're not a veteran canner, follow the directions for heat canning in any reputable manual. The U.S. Food and Drug Administration (FDA) also has directions on its website.

6 cups (1.2 kg) diced watermelon rind (white part only), from an 8-pound (3.6 kg) melon

1 tablespoon baking soda

1 cup (240 ml) water

2½ cups (500 g) sugar

6 cloves

1 cinnamon stick, broken in half

1 bay leaf

A 4-inch (10 cm) strip of lemon zest

Juice of 1 lemon

Place the watermelon rind in a large bowl, cover it with water, and stir in the baking soda. Chill in the fridge for at least 12 hours and up to 24. When you're ready to proceed, drain and rinse and set aside.

In a large pot, combine the water and sugar and bring to a boil over medium heat, stirring to dissolve the sugar. Add the drained watermelon rind, cloves, cinnamon, bay leaf, lemon peel, and lemon juice.

Simmer, stirring now and then, until the rind is translucent and the syrup is thick, 45 to 55 minutes. Meanwhile, prepare your canning jars. When the rind is done, spoon it with its syrup into the hot, sterilized jars, wipe off the rims with a wet cloth, screw on the lids, and turn upside down to cool completely. Store at room temperature for up to a year.

hazelnut, sesame, cacao nib, and orange peel toffee

CUBBAITA

◆◆◆

Makes about 2 pounds (1 kg)

◆◆◆

"Scruscio ri carta e cubbaita nenti" (literally "rustling of paper and no *cubbaita*") is a Sicilian proverb meaning something like "all style and no substance." *Cubbaita* is the honey-almond toffee that has been around since long before the ninth-century Saracens gave it its name, from the Arabic *qubbayt*. Once upon a time, it came wrapped in squares of paper to keep in your pocket, like an OG energy bar. I imagine if you were to find just the paper without the cubbaita, it would be as disappointing as encountering someone or something that's all style and no substance.

There are variations on this theme. *Giuggulena* is the same sugar-and-honey base but made with sesame seeds alone; *petramennula*, or "almond rock," contains orange or lemon zest; and *petrafennula* is pistachio with orange or lemon.

This is sort of a mixtape of all three. There are hazelnuts (and/or almonds), sesame seeds, *and* candied orange peel, with raw cacao nibs added as a bitter, chocolatey counterbalance to all the sweetness—and as a nod to the chocolate of Modica.

One caveat: don't try to make this on a humid day; it'll be sticky and won't harden completely.

2 tablespoons canola, sunflower, or other neutral oil, plus more for the pan

2 cups (250 g) roasted hazelnuts or almonds, or a combination of the two

¾ cup (100 g) toasted sesame seeds

1¼ cups (250 g) sugar

½ cup (120 ml) water

3 tablespoons honey

Juice of half a lemon

½ cup (50 g) finely chopped candied orange peel (page 210)

½ cup (60 g) raw cacao nibs

Flaky sea salt

Preheat the oven to 300°F (150°C). Rub a thin film of flavorless oil onto a rimmed baking sheet and set aside. Place the hazelnuts and sesame seeds on another rimmed baking sheet and warm them in the preheated oven while you caramelize the sugar.

In a large, heavy saucepan over medium-low heat, stir together the sugar, water, honey, lemon juice, and the 2 tablespoons of oil. Stir with a wooden spoon until all of the sugar is dissolved but the mixture isn't yet boiling. Now remove the spoon and don't put it back in until I tell you to. Turn up the heat to medium-high and boil, swirling the pan every now and then so the syrup cooks evenly. After about 10 minutes, it will begin to turn brown and thicken.

With your wooden spoon, stir until the mixture reaches 300°F (150°C) on a candy thermometer. It will be the color of a paper bag. Take the warm sesame seeds and hazelnuts out of the oven and add them, the orange peel, and the cacao nibs to the pan. Stir for a minute or two more, until the mixture reaches 320°F (160°C), then turn it out carefully onto the prepared baking sheet. Rub a metal spatula with a bit of oil and use it to pat the cubbaita into an even layer, about ¼ inch (6 mm) thick. Sprinkle with flaky sea salt. Score the cubbaita into manageable sizes with a sharp knife while it's still warm, then break apart when it's completely cool. Store airtight at room temperature for up to a month.

DRINKS & Liqueurs

BEVANDE E LIQUORI

frothy iced coffee

CAFFÈ FREDDO

◆◆◆

Makes 1 serving at a time

◆◆◆

There is a little *bottega* in New York called Best Sicily, where you can buy Sicilian products and eat Sicilian street food. Nicolas, who runs the place, is from Salemi, where his family still lives. On a recent trip to Sicily, I visited his parents, Franca and Franco, along with the team photographing this book. It was a hot late-summer night, and Franca made *caponata,* a celery-leaf frittata, handmade *busiate* pasta, Franco's homemade sausage, cannoli from scratch, and this frothy iced coffee. I'll never make iced coffee any other way. Don't throw away your coffee grounds either. Use them to fertilize your plants or mix them with a little olive oil and use it as a pre-sun exfoliant, then rinse with cool water and apply sunscreen.

You'll need to start this a day before you plan to serve it, and you'll need to have a clean, empty wine bottle on hand.

12 shots espresso, or 1½ cups (360 ml) brewed espresso

Another shot of freshly brewed espresso

½ teaspoon sugar

Pour the 12 shots of espresso into a clean, empty wine bottle and let it cool to room temperature. Then tilt the bottle in the freezer as horizontally as you can without the coffee spilling out, and freeze overnight, or until solid.

When you're ready to make the iced coffee, stir together the freshly brewed espresso shot and the sugar and pour it into the bottle. Cap or cork the bottle and shake it vigorously until a rich foam forms and the coffee inside is uniformly cold, about 30 seconds.

Pour into an espresso cup or a small glass and drink right away. You can continue with more freshly brewed shots, but shake them one at a time or they won't get frothy. Refreeze the bottle for the next batch. When there are only a few ounces of frozen espresso left, defrost it, dilute with an equal amount of water and feed it to your roses. Wash the bottle and begin the whole operation again.

pistachio milk

LATTE DI PISTACCHIO

◆◆◆

Makes
1 quart (1 L)

◆◆◆

Among the many things I'm surprised I don't see in Sicily (along with nopales, tahini, pomegranate molasses, and stuffed grape leaves) is pistachio milk. It's thick, rich, and a beautiful green color when made with pistachios from Bronte, though any good-quality pistachios will work.

When you are done straining the milk from the ground pistachios, don't throw away the pulp; you can add it to your meatball mix instead of breadcrumbs. (It also makes a good body scrub: spread it out on a baking sheet and leave it to dry, then mix it with a little honey and olive oil. Keep it in the fridge when you're not using it.)

2½ cups (300 g) shelled raw pistachios

4 cups (1 L) filtered water

Pinch of fine sea salt

In a large bowl, combine the pistachios, water, and salt, and chill for at least 8 but no more than 12 hours.

This next part is a little fiddly, but it's worth the effort. Strain the soaking water directly into the jar of an electric blender (use a high-speed blender if you have one) and pour the soaked pistachios out onto a large cotton towel. Rub the pistachios in the towel to remove as many of the loose papery skins as possible. Transfer the skinned pistachios to the blender jar with the water, and blend until the pistachios are pulverized and the milk is thick and creamy, about a minute.

Line a strainer with a white cotton pillowcase or a flour-sack towel, place it over a large bowl, and pour in the contents of the blender, solids and all. When most of the liquid has drained into the bowl, gather up the towel and twist it as tightly as possible, squeezing out all the milk you can into the bowl.

Store in an airtight container and refrigerate; the pistachio milk will keep for up to 3 days.

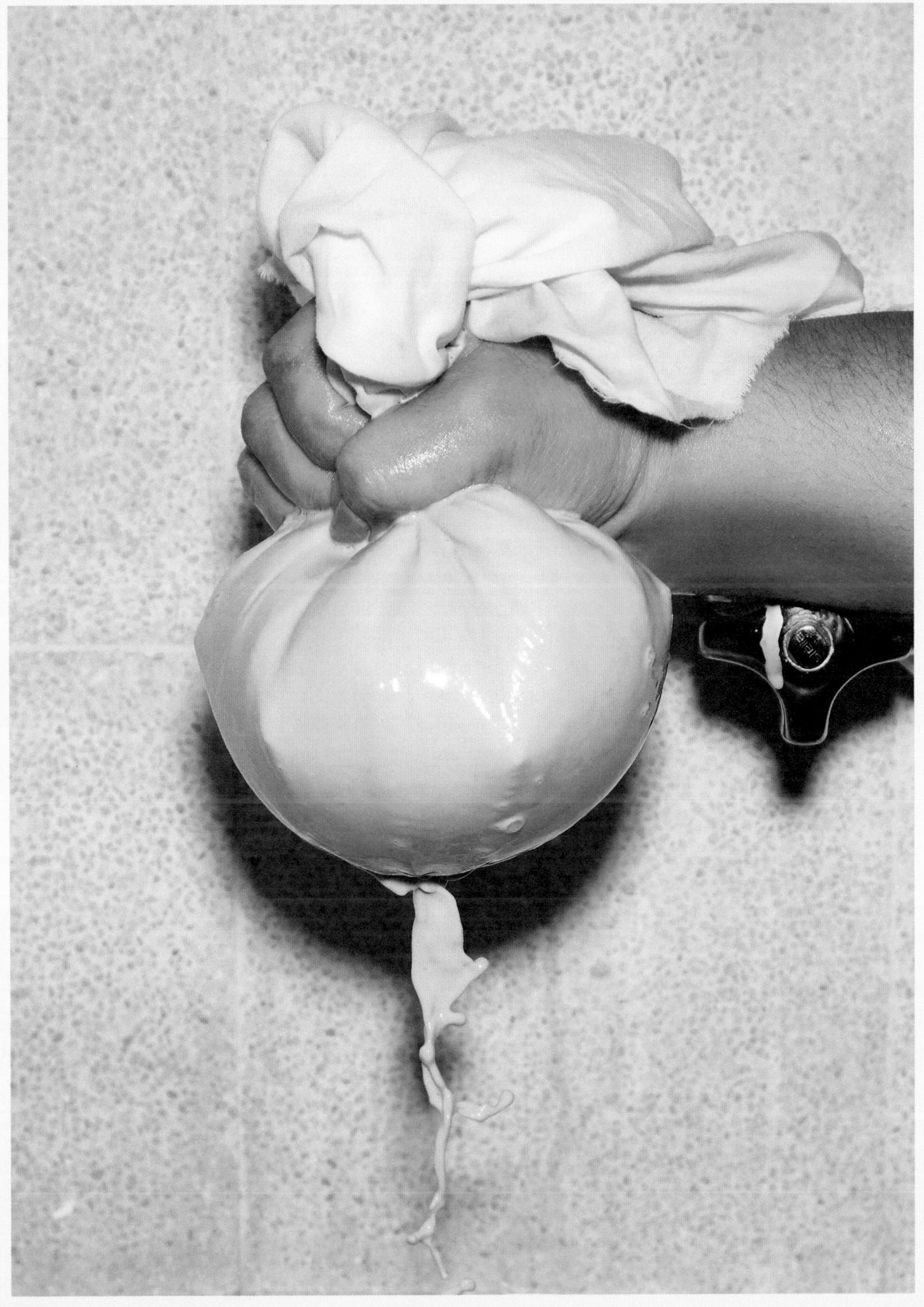

almond milk

LATTE DI MANDORLA

◆◆◆

Makes 1 quart (1 L)

◆◆◆

In Sicily, there are sweet almonds and bitter almonds. The sweet ones taste faintly like a drop of good almond extract. The bitter ones taste boldly of almond extract. I sometimes like a bit of that boldness in my almond milk, so I add bitter almonds, or one of the following options.

Bitter almonds are illegal in the U.S.; they contain a natural toxin that the body breaks down into cyanide. They're fair game in Sicily, however, where everyone knows that the ideal almond flavor comes from using no more than 10 percent bitter to 90 percent sweet almonds.

But there are ways around the bitter-almond prohibition if you want to give your almond milk a more pronounced almond flavor. First, if you happen to be in Northern California, bitter-almond trees grow wild, often in parks or on city property. Second, Chinese herb stores have them; they're boiled and drunk as a tea to treat coughs. From either source, you only need a few of the nuts—remember the 90/10 sweet/bitter rule, and you'll be fine.

Another option for adding depth of flavor to your almond milk is to use a few apricot kernels. These are sold at Middle Eastern groceries (including online ones) as sweet apricot kernels. Or you can pop open a fresh apricot and crack the pit with a hammer; the apricot kernel is inside. Take a little nibble to test for bitterness. Some apricots have sweet kernels, some have bitter ones, but either way, even a few will give you that nice almond flavor. Don't worry about that pesky cyanide; you'd need to drink about five quarts of almond milk at a sitting to even start to feel anything. I've never heard of a Sicilian dropping dead from a glass of almond milk, but you decide for yourself.

2 cups (250 g) blanched almonds

2 tablespoons apricot kernels, or use additional blanched almonds

Pinch of fine sea salt

4 cups (1 L) filtered water

In a large bowl, combine the almonds, apricot kernels, salt, and water and chill for at least 8 but no more than 12 hours. Transfer the almonds and their water to a blender (high speed, if you have one) and blend until the almonds are pulverized and the milk is thick and creamy.

Line a strainer with a white cotton pillowcase or a flour-sack towel, place it over a large bowl, and pour in the contents of the blender, solids and all. When most of the liquid has drained into the bowl, gather up the towel and twist it as tightly as possible, squeezing out all the milk you can into the bowl.

Store, covered, in a glass jar or pitcher and refrigerate; the almond milk will keep for up to 3 days.

grape must syrup

MOSTO COTTO

Makes
2 cups (480 ml)

Mosto cotto is an ancient sweetener, as old as wine. Grape must—the freshly pressed juice from wine grapes, still containing some seeds and skin—is cooked down until the sugars have concentrated and the must becomes a thick syrup.

For the greater part of 800 years, Sicily operated under a feudal system, wherein the aristocracy owned and controlled much of the land and the peasants worked it. When it was time for the *vendemmia*, or grape harvest, landowners got the good grapes, and the inferior, sour ones were given to the peasants. They in turn figured out how to sweeten the must by cooking it with the ash of burnt grapevines, whose alkalinity would increase the pH of the juice, effectively sweetening it without adding sugar. Often, chunks of apple or quince, figs, bergamot, or mandarin peels were added to improve the flavor. Use mosto cotto in place of sugar, honey, molasses, or maple syrup.

1 cup (125 g) wood ash, from burned grapevines or your local wood-burning pizzeria

5 pounds (2¼ kg) wine grapes, such as Cabernet Sauvignon, Zinfandel, or Merlot, no stems

First, sift the ash to remove any larger bits.

Next, in a large, deep pot, mash the grapes with a potato masher or your hands. You can also pulse them in a food processor until the grapes' skins are broken and the fruit is crushed. Mix the ashes into the grapes in the pot and bring to a simmer over medium heat; don't let it boil. Keep simmering for an hour, occasionally mashing the grapes against the sides of the pot with the spoon to extract as much juice and natural pectin as you can.

Place a mesh strainer over a bowl and ladle in the grape mixture. Discard the solids (or feed them to your roses). Wash the strainer and the pot well, line the strainer with a cotton pillowcase or flour-sack towel, and place it over the pot. Ladle the liquid into the strainer to catch the ashes. Don't press on the strainer or squeeze the cloth; just be patient and let the liquid drain through in its own time. It won't take long. (The ashes can go to your roses too.)

Return the uncovered pot to medium-high heat and bring just to a boil. Lower the heat to medium and simmer it for an hour. After an hour, give it a stir, reduce the heat to low, and continue to cook at the very gentlest simmer. It will take a total of about 2 hours for the liquid to reduce to a syrup the thickness of honey. Don't be tempted to boil it quickly; too much heat and a lack of patience will make a bitter, burnt-tasting mosto cotto. Store in a covered glass jar in the fridge or at room temperature. It will keep indefinitely.

homemade sambuca

ZAMMÙ

◆◆◆

Makes about 6 cups (1.4 L)

◆◆◆

In the days before public health and clean water laws, there were *acquavitari*, or water-sellers, in Palermo. Some operated out of kiosks and some carried their wares on their backs, but all of them dispensed water with a few drops of *zammù* added as a disinfectant (everyone drank out of the same glass). Eventually, people developed a taste for it, with water or without. The word zammù comes from the Latin *sambucus*, or elderberry, which some versions of zammù contain, and one of them became known as the anise-flavored liqueur sambuca. Nowadays, *acqua zammù* is a refreshing drink sold from kiosks all over Palermo. Order a *caffè corretto* in a bar, and you'll get an espresso with a splash of sambuca added to "correct" it.

4 cups (1 L) grain alcohol, such as Everclear or 100-proof vodka

½ cup (75 g) star anise pods

15 whole peppercorns

3 tablespoons fennel seeds

A 2-inch (5 cm) piece of cinnamon stick, broken

1½ cups (300 g) sugar

2 cups (480 ml) water

In a 1-gallon (4 L) jar with a lid, combine the alcohol, star anise, peppercorns, fennel seeds, and cinnamon stick. Cover the jar and set it aside in a cool, dark place for 40 days and 40 nights.

On the forty-first day (or anytime thereafter), bring the sugar and water to a boil in a medium saucepan, stirring to dissolve the sugar. Turn the heat down and simmer for 5 minutes, then allow the syrup to cool completely. Stir the cooled syrup into the alcohol and strain the liquid into bottles, discarding the spices. Zammù keeps at room temperature indefinitely.

elixir of the seven powers

ELISIR DEI SETTE POTENTI

◆◆◆

Makes about 6 cups (1.4 L)

◆◆◆

Sicilian superstitions run deep. The *malocchio*, or evil eye, is a real thing. (I have its antidote tattooed on my arm, just for good measure.) And here is an elixir that is also believed to have powers—seven of them, no less. It's not clear whether the "seven powers" may refer to the seven main ingredients that make up the concoction, or to other secret powers this *elisir* may possess. In any event, I've added an extra ingredient that I believe increases the elixir's metaphysical potency considerably: *coccinella*, or cochineal. These are tiny little insects that infest cactus and have been the source of a brilliant—and eponymous—scarlet dye since before Spanish galleons brought the bugs back from the New World in the sixteenth century. Cochineal is what used to give bitters like Campari and Aperol their red color, and it's readily available online.

Red is a *portafortuna*, or good luck charm, that attracts romance and passion and that wards off the malocchio. You'll often see a red ribbon tied onto a baby's carriage for protection against too many compliments, which could bring on the malocchio.

4 cups (1 L) grain alcohol, such as Everclear or 100-proof vodka

1 cinnamon stick, broken

6 whole cloves

Half a vanilla bean, split lengthwise

3 whole star anise pods

¼ teaspoon saffron threads

3 large stems fresh mint with their leaves

1 tablespoon dried cochineal (optional)

1½ cups (300 g) sugar

2 cups (480 ml) water

In a 1-gallon (4 L) jar with a lid, combine the alcohol, cinnamon, cloves, vanilla bean, star anise, saffron, mint, and cochineal. Cover the jar and set it aside in a cool, dark place for 40 days and 40 nights.

On the forty-first day (or anytime thereafter), bring the sugar and water to a boil in a medium saucepan over medium-high heat, stirring to dissolve the sugar. Turn the heat down and simmer for 5 minutes, then allow to cool completely. Stir this cooled syrup into the alcohol and strain the liquid into bottles, discarding the solids. The elisir keeps at room temperature indefinitely.

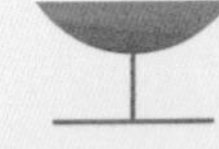

rose-petal and cardamom liqueur

ROSOLIO ALLA ROSA

Makes 6 cups (1.4 L)

You may have noticed Sicilians' fondness for floral essences—rose, orange-blossom, jasmine—and for other things florid, like language, architecture, and dreams. Rose water (definitely a legacy of the Saracens) has an easy affinity for almonds and pistachios and finds its way into cakes, ices, and beverages across the island. Here we have *rosolio,* a very traditional cordial made with rose petals. The name rosolio is thought to derive from *ros* (rose) + *olio* (oil) for its viscosity. But then again, there are rosolios of many flavors that have nothing at all to do with roses, so my own common-sense belief is that rosolio is to liqueurs what Kleenex is to tissues or Xerox is to photocopies. What I do know for sure is that rosolio is made at home and is offered to guests as a *digestivo* (digestive) and a sign of hospitality. To add an optional red tint to this, you can add a teaspoon of cochineal, the tiny little insects that have been the source of a brilliant-scarlet dye since long before Spanish galleons brought them from the New World in the sixteenth century. Cochineal is food-safe and is readily available online.

4 cups (1 L) grain alcohol, such as Everclear or 100-proof vodka

8 cups (600 g) of the most fragrant unsprayed rose petals you can get your hands on

½ to 1 teaspoon cochineal

2 cups (400 g) sugar

2 cups (480 ml) water

2 tablespoons rose water, if your rose petals don't taste rosy enough

In a 1-gallon (4 L) jar with a lid, combine the alcohol, rose petals, and cochineal. Cover the jar and set it aside in a cool, dark place for 40 days and 40 nights.

On the forty-first day (or anytime thereafter), bring the sugar and water to a boil in a medium saucepan over medium-high heat, stirring to dissolve the sugar. Turn the heat down and simmer for 5 minutes, then whisk in the rose water, if using, and allow to cool completely. Stir the cooled syrup into the alcohol and strain the liquid into bottles, discarding the solids. The rosolio keeps at room temperature indefinitely.

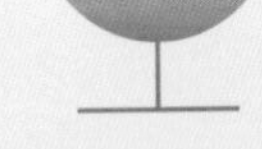

citrus liqueur

LIQUORE AGLI AGRUMI

◆◆◆

Makes about 7 cups (1.75 L)

◆◆◆

You've probably heard of *limoncello*. This is that, but using lots of citrus, not just lemons. It becomes a lot more interesting when you mix things up a bit, using as many different types of citrus as you like. A nice thing about citrus fruits is that, unlike Sicilians, they don't clash within their own family. Using citrus leaves isn't mandatory, but they do add a fresh herbal note to the finished liqueur.

12 assorted citrus: any combination of lemons, limes, mandarins, oranges, bergamot, grapefruit, calamansi to total 3 pounds (1.4 kg)

8 unsprayed leaves from any of the citrus (optional)

4 cups (1 L) grain alcohol, such as Everclear or 100-proof vodka

1½ cups (300 g) sugar

2 cups (480 ml) water

First, peel all the zest from all of the citrus with a vegetable peeler. Try to get just the zest, not any of the white pith. Crush the leaves (if using) in your hands to release the oils. Transfer the zest, along with the leaves and the alcohol, to a 1-gallon (4 L) jar with a lid. Cover the jar and set it aside in a cool, dark place for 40 days and 40 nights.

On the forty-first day (or anytime thereafter), bring the sugar and water to a boil in a medium saucepan over medium-high heat, stirring to dissolve the sugar. Turn the heat down and simmer for 5 minutes, then allow to cool completely. Stir the cooled syrup into the alcohol and strain it into bottles, discarding the solids. The liquore keeps at room temperature indefinitely.

green herbal liqueur

LIQUORI ALLE ERBE

◆◆◆

Makes about 7 cups (1.75 L)

◆◆◆

The thing about alcohol is that it pulls out all the individual flavor notes added to it and presents them in layers—just like perfume—for us to experience one by one. The result is that each of these three liqueurs tastes not only like more than the sum of its parts, but like every flavor note of each of the parts as well. Bay leaf liqueur—*alloro*—has notes of pine and eucalyptus; *basilico*, or basil liqueur, tastes of mint, pepper, and cinnamon; and *finocchietto*, or fennel liqueur, gifts us with licorice, mint, and honey. Each of these liqueurs begins life with a vivid green color that mellows to a light amber with time. For myself, I like an after-dinner digestive of finocchietto with a spritz of fizzy water.

4 cups (1 L) grain alcohol, such as Everclear or 100-proof vodka

30 fresh bay leaves or 3 ounces (85 g) basil leaves and stems or 3 ounces (85 g) wild *finocchio* (fennel) fronds

1½ cups (300 g) sugar

2 cups (480 ml) water

Pour the alcohol into a 1-gallon (4 L) jar with a lid. Add the herb of your choice. Cover the jar and set it aside in a cool, dark place for 40 days and 40 nights.

On the forty-first day (or anytime thereafter), bring the sugar and water to a boil in a medium saucepan over medium-high heat, stirring to dissolve the sugar. Turn the heat down and simmer for 5 minutes, then allow to cool completely. Stir the cooled syrup into the alcohol and strain it into bottles, discarding the solids. The liquore keeps at room temperature indefinitely.

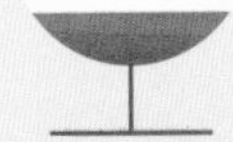

7
ITALA
PILSEN
BIRRA SUPERIORE

ACKNOWLEDGMENTS

You were with me in 1995 when I read that first story about Maria Grammatico; you were there for the trips to Sicily to work on my first book; and you've been there for the entire journey of the making of this one. Without your keen eye, discerning palate, wise counsel, and ability to (a) navigate both the confounding Sicilian motorways and my mercurial temperament while (b) finding supreme irony in nearly everything, this book would never have happened. Thank you, Monica May, star in your own right and dear friend, for everything. You kept our little team going with your humor, wisdom, and bountiful plates of home-cooked pasta.

Louise Hagger, not only did you capture the beauty of Sicily in your photos, you captured her soul and her spirit. Thank you for your patience, your grit, your exquisite taste, and your good cheer. You are a kind and gentle soul, with immense talent, moxie, and grace. Thank you.

Thank you also to Sophie Bronze. We could not have done this without you. (Well, maybe we could have, but it would have taken twice as long and been half as fun). Thank you, Ester Masciocchi, *cara amica*, for coordinating our appointments, for tasting all my recipe trials and failures, and for your artful eye and your calm spirit. You too, Luca Vergano. Huge thanks to my agent Martha Hopkins for being so freaking smart—and for getting this out into the world. Next trip, you're coming with! Janet Paist, *gioia mia,* thank you for tasting, talking, editing, and schlepping down from Rome to join our little team. Thank you, Shannon Dowling, for your recipe wrangling. Thank you to Theo, *fichiu miu,* for using your parkour skills to get us back into the *baglio* and for your production assistance. And to my editor Jenny Wapner, an immense, heartfelt, sweet chunk of gratitude to you for giving this book life.

Tante Belle Cose

to you all!

INDEX

◆◆◆

A

Agatha, Saint, 1, 68, 82, 96
Agrigento, 25
Alfio Neri, 106
Alhambra Decree, 7
almond flour, 21
  Almond Blossoms, 66
  Almond Cookies with Sugared Anise Seeds or Pine Nuts, 67
  Almond Eyes of Saint Lucy, 78
  Almond Sweetmeats, 71–73
  Apple and Thyme Honey Cake with Toasted Fennel and Almonds, 144
  Baked Almond Bonbons, 69
  Cooked Marzipan, 62
  Fig and Olive Shortbreads, 52
  Lemon- and Fennel-Scented Almond Biscotti, 43
  The Leopard's Almond Cookies, 70
  Little Almond and Cherry Cookies, 75–77
  Modican Chocolate and Meat Pastries, 102
  Saint Agatha's Little Olives, 68
  Spiced Chocolate Cookies, 44
  Sun-Dried Tomato and Anise Shortbreads, 54
almonds, 24–25
  Almond Milk, 224
  Almond-Milk Cremolata, 182
  Almond-Milk Pudding with Roasted Apricots, 173
  bitter, 25, 224
  Cooked Marzipan, 62
  Lemon- and Fennel-Scented Almond Biscotti, 43
  Mandarin Orange–Almond Cookies, 90–93
  Spiced Fig and Chocolate Christmas Cookies, 85–86
  Spiced Mosto Cotto Cookies, 50
  Sun-Dried Wine Grape Confection, 206
ammonium carbonate, 22
anasini, 67
anginetti, 48
anise, 23
  Almond Cookies with Sugared Anise Seeds or Pine Nuts, 67
  Anisette Toasts, 36
  Elixir of the Seven Powers, 227
  Homemade Sambuca, 226
  Lemon-Anise Pastries for Easter and Purim, 118
  Sun-Dried Tomato and Anise Shortbreads, 54
Antica Dolceria Bonajuto, 100, 102, 174
Apple and Thyme Honey Cake with Toasted Fennel and Almonds, 144
apricot kernels, 25, 224
  Almond Milk, 224
  Cooked Marzipan, 62
Apricots, Roasted, Almond-Milk Pudding with, 173
arancine dolci, 148
Avola, 25

B

baking by eye, 26
baking powder, 22
Bar St. Honoré, 55
basil
  Green Herbal Liqueur, 231
bay
  Green Herbal Liqueur, 231
  Lemon Bergamot Olive Oil Cake, 140-42
  mostarda di uva, 206
  Quince Paste, 203-5
beef
  Modican Chocolate and Meat Pastries, 102
Benedictine Chocolate Pudding, 174–75
bergamot
  Citrus Liqueur, 230
  Lemon Bergamot Olive Oil Cake, 140–42
Best Sicily, 220
biancomangiare con albicocche arrostite, 173
bignè, 113–15
biscotti a esse, 38
biscotti all'anice, 36
biscotti al latte, 34
biscotti ricci del gattopardo, 70
blackberries
  Almond Sweetmeats, 71–73
  Etna Mess, 74
Bonbons, Baked Almond, 69
Breakfast Braids, 35
brioche col tuppo, 150–51
Bronte, 25, 27, 94, 185, 212
Bufalini, Gesualdo, 96
Buns, Sweet Yeast, 150–51
butter, 22

C

cacao nibs
Hazelnut, Sesame, Cacao Nib, and Orange Peel Toffee, 216
caffè freddo, 220
Caffè Sicilia, 144, 182
cakes
Apple and Thyme Honey Cake with Toasted Fennel and Almonds, 144
Baked Ricotta and Tart Cherry Torte, 136
Cassata in the Style of Tiramisu, 132
Chocolate Hazelnut Layer Cake, 145
Lemon Bergamot Olive Oil Cake, 140–42
Little Cassatas, 82
Mandarin-Pistachio Ring Cake, 143
Ricotta Cheesecake for Passover, 134
Sponge Cake, 133
Cannoli, 106–7, 110
cardamom
Coffee and Cardamom Granita, 180
Rose-Petal and Cardamom Liqueur, 229
cassata
Cassata in the Style of Tiramisu, 132
history of, 128
Little Cassatas, 82
cassata al forno, 136
cassata finta, 132
cassatedde Partinico, 157
cassatine, 82
Catania, 1, 8, 17, 68, 82, 96, 148, 174, 203
cherries
Baked Ricotta and Tart Cherry Torte, 136
Little Almond and Cherry Cookies, 75–77
Little Cassatas, 82
Ricotta-Filled Puffs for Saint Joseph's Day, 158–59
Ricotta Pastries for Saint Agatha, 96
chiacchiere, 112
Chickpea Turnovers, Sweet, 157
chocolate, 100
Almond Sweetmeats, 71–73
Benedictine Chocolate Pudding, 174–75
Chocolate Cremolata, 184
Chocolate Custard Filling, 166
Chocolate-Filled Pastry Puffs, 116
Chocolate Hazelnut Layer Cake, 145
Frozen Chocolate and Hazelnut Praline Cream, 188–89
Modican Chocolate and Meat Pastries, 102
Ricotta-Filled Doughnuts, 154–56
Rustic Tart at Your Whim, 137
Spiced Chocolate Cookies, 44
Spiced Fig and Chocolate Christmas Cookies, 85–86
Sweet Chickpea Turnovers, 157
Sweetened Ricotta Cream, 164
Watermelon Pudding, 168
Choux Pastry Puffs, 113–15
ciambella al mandarino e pistacchio, 143
cinnamon, 23
citrus fruits
Citrus Liqueur, 230
See also individual fruits
Clinton, Bill, 66
cloves, 23
cochineal, 227
Elixir of the Seven Powers, 227
Rose-Petal and Cardamom Liqueur, 229
coffee
Coffee and Cardamom Granita, 180
Frothy Iced Coffee, 220
confettura di fragole, 197
confettura di pesche Settembrine cotte al sole, 200
confettura di pomodori e foglie di limone, 202
convent sweets, 120, 124
cookies
Almond Blossoms, 66
Almond Cookies with Sugared Anise Seeds or Pine Nuts, 67
Anisette Toasts, 36
Breakfast Braids, 35
Fig and Olive Shortbreads, 52
Hazelnut and Orange Meringues, 55
Iced Lemon Rings, 48
Lemon- and Fennel-Scented Almond Biscotti, 43
The Leopard's Almond Cookies, 70
Little Almond and Cherry Cookies, 75–77
Mandarin Orange–Almond Cookies, 90–93
Milk Biscuits, 34
Pistachio-Filled Holiday Cookies, 94
Queen's Biscuits, 37
"S" Cookies, 38
Soft Cookie Clouds, 49
Spiced Chocolate Cookies, 44
Spiced Fig and Chocolate Christmas Cookies, 85–86
Spiced Mosto Cotto Cookies, 50
Sun-Dried Tomato and Anise Shortbreads, 54
Costanza d'Aragona, Queen of Sicily, 136
cotognata, 203–5
crema al cioccolato, 166
crema al pistacchio, 165
crema di ricotta, 164
crema pasticcera, 165
cremolata
Almond-Milk Cremolata, 182
Chocolate Cremolata, 184
Pistachio Milk Cremolata, 185
cremolata alle mandorle, 182
cremolata di cioccolato, 184
cremolata di pistachio, 185
croccantini al nocciole e arancia candite, 55

crostata capricciosa, 137
cubbaita, 216
cuccidati, 85
cucuzza, 215

D
dolci di badia, 120, 124
dolcini da riposto, 71
dolcini di Erice, 71
Donnafugata, 70
Doughnuts, Ricotta-Filled, 154–56
drinks and liqueurs
  Almond Milk, 224
  Citrus Liqueur, 230
  Elixir of the Seven Powers, 227
  Frothy Iced Coffee, 220
  Green Herbal Liqueur, 231
  Homemade Sambuca, 226
  Pistachio Milk, 222
  Rose-Petal and Cardamom Liqueur, 229

E
elisir dei sette potenti, 227
Elixir of the Seven Powers, 227
Erice, 8, 71, 87
Etna, Mount, 25, 144, 185, 196, 212
Etna Mess, 74
extracts, 23

F
fennel, 23
  Apple and Thyme Honey Cake with Toasted Fennel and Almonds, 144
  Green Herbal Liqueur, 231
  Lemon- and Fennel-Scented Almond Biscotti, 43
  Lemon, Raisin, and Fennel Seed Fritters, 160
Ferdinand, King of Naples and Sicily, 17, 113
Ferdinand, King of Spain, 7
figs, 24
  Fig and Olive Shortbreads, 52
  Spiced Fig and Chocolate Christmas Cookies, 85–86
  Sun-Dried Wine Grape Confection, 206
finta zuccata candita, 215
fior di mandorla, 66
fiori di Sicilia, 23
flours, 21
frittelle di San Martino, 160
fritters
  Lemon, Raisin, and Fennel Seed Fritters, 160
  Sweet Rice Fritters, 148
frollini ai fichi e olive, 52
frollini al pomodori secchi e anice, 54
frutta martorana, 58

G
Garibaldi, Giuseppe, 17
gattò di ricotta, 128, 134
gelati, ordering, 190
gelo di cioccolato, 174–75
gelo di melone, 168
genovesi, 87–88
giuggulena, 216
Goethe, Johann Wolfgang von, 9
Grammatico, Maria, 8, 9, 87
granita al caffè turco, 180
granita al limone, 179
granite
  Coffee and Cardamom Granita, 180
  Lemon Ice Scented with Lemon Leaves, 179
  ordering, 193
  See also cremolata
grapes
  Grape Must Syrup, 225
  Spiced Mosto Cotto Cookies, 50
  Sun-Dried Wine Grape Confection, 206
Green Herbal Liqueur, 231

H
hazelnuts, 25
  Chocolate Hazelnut Layer Cake, 145
  Frozen Chocolate and Hazelnut Praline Cream, 188–89
  Hazelnut and Orange Meringues, 55
  Hazelnut, Sesame, Cacao Nib, and Orange Peel Toffee, 216
honey, 144
  Apple and Thyme Honey Cake with Toasted Fennel and Almonds, 144
Hyblaean Mountains, 144

I
impanatigghe, 102
Iris, 154
Isabella, Queen of Spain, 7

J
jams. *See* preserves
Joseph, Saint, 158

L
ladyfingers
  Cassata in the Style of Tiramisu, 132
Lampedusa, Giuseppe Tomasi di, 1, 70, 120
lard, 22
latte di mandorla, 224
latte di pistacchio, 222
lemons
  Citrus Liqueur, 230
  Iced Lemon Rings, 48
  Lemon- and Fennel-Scented Almond Biscotti, 43
  Lemon-Anise Pastries for Easter and Purim, 118
  Lemon Bergamot Olive Oil Cake, 140–42
  Lemon Ice Scented with Lemon Leaves, 179
  Lemon, Raisin, and Fennel Seed Fritters, 160
  Little Almond and Cherry Cookies, 75–77
  "S" Cookies, 38
  Sweet Tomato and Lemon Leaf Preserves, 202
The Leopard's Almond Cookies, 70
Lipari, 50, 90
liqueurs. *See* drinks and liqueurs
liquore agli agrumi, 230
liquori alle erbe, 231
I Lochi, 27, 185
Lo Verso, Antonio, 154
Lucy, Saint, 78

M
Madonie, 25
Mandarin Orange–Almond Cookies, 90–93
mandarins
  Citrus Liqueur, 230
  Mandarin Orange–Almond Cookies, 90–93
  Mandarin-Pistachio Ring Cake, 143
Maraini, Dacia, 125
Margherita, Queen of Savoy, 37
Maria Carolina, Queen of Naples and Sicily, 17, 113
marmalades. *See* preserves
marmellata di arance rosse e rose, 196
Martin, Saint, 160
Martorana, Goffredo and Eloisa, 58
marzapane (marzipan)
  Cooked Marzipan, 62
  frutta martorana, 58
  Little Cassatas, 82
Mascagni, Pietro, 154
Mazara del Vallo, 16, 69, 168
measuring, 26
Meringues, Hazelnut and Orange, 55
Messina, 180, 193
Milazzo, 50
Milk Biscuits, 34
minne di Sant'Agata, 82, 96
Modica, 21, 71, 100, 102, 174, 216
Molino di Santa Maria, 21
Monte Erei, 49
Monteleone, 85
mostarda di uva, 206
mosto cotto, 225
  Spiced Mosto Cotto Cookies, 50
muccunetti, 69
mulberries
  Almond Sweetmeats, 71–73
  Etna Mess, 74

N
nacatuli brontesi, 94
nacatuli eoliani, 90–93
Nebrodi, 25
Neri, Francesco, 106
Noto, 8, 144, 176, 182, 203
nuvolette, 49

O
gli occhi di Santa Lucia, 78
oils, 22
ojos de Haman, 118
Oliveri, Maria, 124, 128
olives
  Fig and Olive Shortbreads, 52
  oil, 22
olivette di Sant'Agata, 68
orange-blossom water, 23
oranges
  Almond Eyes of Saint Lucy, 78
  Almond Sweetmeats, 71–73
  Baked Almond Bonbons, 69
  Blood Orange and Rose Water Marmalade, 196
  Candied Orange Peel, 210
  Citrus Liqueur, 230
  Cream-Filled Pastries, 87–88
  Hazelnut and Orange Meringues, 55
  Hazelnut, Sesame, Cacao Nib, and Orange Peel Toffee, 216
  Pomegranate and Orange Pudding, 172
  See also mandarins

P
Paladino, Luigi, 27, 185
Palermo, 17, 58, 69, 71, 113, 124, 128, 136, 148, 154, 157, 168, 203, 226
Pallavicini, Marchese, 133
Palma di Montechiaro, 69, 70
pan di Spagna, 133
panino di Santa Caterina, 69
Pantelleria, 24

Partinico, 157
pasta di pistacchio, 212
pasta frolla, 135
pasta reale, 58, 62
Pasticceria F.lli Gangi, 185
Pasticceria Maria Grammatico, 87
Pasticceria Russo, 58, 68
Pasticceria Subba, 90
pasticcini alle mandorle e amarena, 75–77
pasticciona dell'Etna, 74
pastries
  Chocolate-Filled Pastry Puffs, 116
  Choux Pastry Puffs, 113–15
  Cream-Filled Pastries, 87–88
  Crispy Pastry Strips, 112
  Lemon-Anise Pastries for Easter and Purim, 118
  Little Cassatas, 82
  Modican Chocolate and Meat Pastries, 102
  Ricotta-Filled Puffs for Saint Joseph's Day, 158–59
  Ricotta Pastries for Saint Agatha, 96
  Sweet Chickpea Turnovers, 157
  Sweet Pastry Dough, 135
Pastry Cream, 165
peaches
  Late-Harvest Sun-Cooked Peach Preserves, 200
  Rustic Tart at Your Whim, 137
petrafennula, 216
petramennula, 216
Piana degli Albanesi, 106
pignoli amaretti, 67
Pine Nuts, Almond Cookies with, 67
pistachio flour, 21
  Breakfast Braids, 35
  The Leopard's Almond Cookies, 70
  Mandarin-Pistachio Ring Cake, 143
pistachios, 25, 27
  Cassata in the Style of Tiramisu, 132
  Cream-Filled Pastries, 87–88
  Etna Mess, 74
  Pistachio Butter, 212
  Pistachio-Filled Holiday Cookies, 94
  Pistachio Milk, 222
  Pistachio Milk Cremolata, 185
  Sweetened Pistachio Cream, 165
pizzicaloru, 90
Pomegranate and Orange Pudding, 172
preserves
  Blood Orange and Rose Water Marmalade, 196
  Late-Harvest Sun-Cooked Peach Preserves, 200
  Quince Paste, 203–5
  Strawberry Jam Made with Homemade Pectin, 197
  Sweet Tomato and Lemon Leaf Preserves, 202
puddings
  Almond-Milk Pudding with Roasted Apricots, 173
  Benedictine Chocolate Pudding, 174–75
  Pomegranate and Orange Pudding, 172
  Purceddu Melon and Mint Pudding, 169
  Watermelon Pudding, 168
pupi cu l'ova, 118
pupi di zucchero, 44, 47, 48
Purceddu Melon and Mint Pudding, 169

Q

quaresimali, 43
Queen's Biscuits, 37
Quince Paste, 203–5

R

raisins, 24
  Lemon, Raisin, and Fennel Seed Fritters, 160
raspberries
  Etna Mess, 74
reginelle, 37
Rice Fritters, Sweet, 148
ricotta
  Baked Ricotta and Tart Cherry Torte, 136
  Cannoli, 106–7
  Cassata in the Style of Tiramisu, 132
  Little Cassatas, 82
  Ricotta Cheesecake for Passover, 134
  Ricotta-Filled Doughnuts, 154–56
  Ricotta-Filled Puffs for Saint Joseph's Day, 158–59
  Ricotta Pastries for Saint Agatha, 96
  Rustic Tart at Your Whim, 137
  Sweetened Ricotta Cream, 164
Rosalia, Saint, 168
rose petals
  Little Almond and Cherry Cookies, 75–77
  Rose-Petal and Cardamom Liqueur, 229
rose water, 23
rosolio alla rosa, 229
Ruta family, 100, 174

S

saffron
  Elixir of the Seven Powers, 227
  Little Almond and Cherry Cookies, 75–77
Saint Agatha's Little Olives, 68
Salemi, 128, 134, 220
salt, 22
Sambuca, Homemade, 226
San Cataldo, 49
Santa Venerina, 58
Santo Stefano, 203
Schillirò, Biagio, 27
Sciurcia, Giuseppe, 47
"S" Cookies, 38

scorza d'arancia candita, 210
I Segreti del Chiostro, 69, 71, 124, 128
semifreddo al croccante, 188–89
semolina flour, 21
sesame seeds, 25
  Breakfast Braids, 35
  Hazelnut, Sesame, Cacao Nib, and Orange Peel Toffee, 216
  Queen's Biscuits, 37
sfinci di San Giuseppe, 158–59
shortening, 22
Sicily
  expulsion of Jews from, 7, 17
  food culture of, 9, 12, 16
  monasteries and convents in, 124, 174
  sights of, 8–9
  timeline for, 16–17
Siracusa, 16, 78, 106
sospiri di monaca, 71–73
spicchiteddi, 50
Sponge Cake, 133
strawberries
  Almond Sweetmeats, 71–73
  Strawberry Jam Made with Homemade Pectin, 197

T

Taormina, 8, 55, 66
taralli al limone, 48
Tart, Rustic, at Your Whim, 137
teio al limone, 44
testa di turco, 116
tetù al limone, 48
tetù e teio, 44
Toffee, Hazelnut, Sesame, Cacao Nib, and Orange Peel, 216
tomatoes
  Sun-Dried Tomato and Anise Shortbreads, 54
  Sweet Tomato and Lemon Leaf Preserves, 202
torta all'olio di oliva, limone, e bergamotto, 140–42
torta mele-miele, 144
torta Savoia, 145
Trapani, 16, 22, 87
treccine, 35
trionfo di gola, 125
Turnovers, Sweet Chickpea, 157

V

vanilla, 23
vodka
  Citrus Liqueur, 230
  Elixir of the Seven Powers, 227
  Green Herbal Liqueur, 231
  Homemade Sambuca, 226
  Rose-Petal and Cardamom Liqueur, 229

W

walnuts
  Spiced Fig and Chocolate Christmas Cookies, 85–86
watermelon
  Baked Almond Bonbons, 69
  Preserved Watermelon Rind in the Style of Zuccata, 215
  Watermelon Pudding, 168
white chocolate
  Sweetened Pistachio Cream, 165

Z

zammù, 226
zuccata, 215

Hardie Grant North America
2912 Telegraph Ave
Berkeley, CA 94705
hardiegrantusa.com

Published in the United States by Hardie Grant North America, an imprint of Hardie Grant Publishing Pty Ltd.

Library of Congress Cataloging-in-Publication Data is available upon request.

ISBN: 9781958417492
ISBN: 9781958417508 (eBook)

Printed in China
Design by Evi-O.Studio | Evi O. & Susan Le
Prop and Food styling by Victoria Granof
First Edition

Hardie Grant
NORTH AMERICA

MIX
Paper | Supporting responsible forestry
FSC® C020056

Victoria Granof was named one of the most creative and inspiring women in food by *Cherry Bombe*, and a woman to follow by The Spruce Eats. She is one of today's most visionary and vibrant culinary artists. Her loyal clients include *Martha Stewart Living*, *Food & Wine*, *Vogue*, *Rachael Ray Everyday*, Delish, *Bon Appétit*, Food52, *Epicurious*, *Wall Street Journal*, *New York Magazine*, and the *New York Times*. She is the author of four cookbooks and is based in Brooklyn, New York.